TRACY TAYLOR

The Complete Emergency Preparedness Guide

First published by Prince of Pages, Inc. 2025

Copyright © 2025 by Tracy Taylor

All rights reserved. No part of this publication may be reproduced, stored or transmitted in any form or by any means, electronic, mechanical, photocopying, recording, scanning, or otherwise without written permission from the publisher. It is illegal to copy this book, post it to a website, or distribute it by any other means without permission.

Tracy Taylor has no responsibility for the persistence or accuracy of URLs for external or third-party Internet Websites referred to in this publication and does not guarantee that any content on such Websites is, or will remain, accurate or appropriate.

First edition

ISBN: 978-1-949252-54-5

This book was professionally typeset on Reedsy.
Find out more at reedsy.com

Contents

Introduction	1
Why Preparedness Matters More Than Ever	1
Chapter 1	4
Water & Hydration Systems	4
Chapter 2	14
Food & Nutrition Planning	14
Chapter 3	27
Medical & First Aid Preparedness	27
Chapter 4	44
Tools, Repair & Maintenance	44
Chapter 5	63
Lighting, Power & Communications	63
Chapter 6	79
Chapter 6: Shelter & Warmth Management	79
Chapter 7	94
Chapter 7: Hygiene & Sanitation Systems	94
Chapter 8	109
Important Documents & Financial Resources	109
Chapter 9	126
Special Populations & Pets	126
Chapter 10	145
Security & Self-Defense	145
Chapter 11	162
Transportation & Evacuation	162
Chapter 12	179
Planning, Skills & Community Building	179

Chapter 13	199
Resource Optimization & Technology	199
Chapter 14	217
Beyond Basic Preparedness	217
Appendix A	237
Appendix B	261
Appendix C	280
Appendix D	299

Introduction

Why Preparedness Matters More Than Ever

"Whether you're prepping for a hypothetical zombie apocalypse or gearing up for real-world natural disasters, having everything in place ahead of time can save lives and reduce panic."

In an era of increasing natural disasters, infrastructure vulnerabilities, and supply chain disruptions, emergency preparedness has evolved from a niche concern to an essential aspect of life planning. This guide represents a comprehensive approach to building true resilience—not just surviving an emergency, but maintaining comfort, health, and security during prolonged disruptions.

The Modern Reality of Emergency Preparedness

Recent events have demonstrated how quickly our normal systems can be disrupted. Power grids fail during storms, supply chains break down during global crises, and communication networks become overwhelmed during disasters. The families who weather these challenges most successfully aren't necessarily those with the most resources—they're those who planned systematically and prepared thoroughly.

This guide takes you beyond basic emergency kits to build comprehensive family resilience. We'll help you create layered systems that work whether you're dealing with a brief power outage or an extended regional emergency.

How This Guide Works

Systematic Building Blocks: Rather than overwhelming you with massive shopping lists, we break preparedness into logical categories that build on each other. Start with water and food security, then layer in power, communication, and specialized needs.

Real-World Calculations: Every recommendation is sized for practical application. When we suggest storing fifty-six gallons of water for a family of four, we show you exactly how that breaks down (one gallon per person per day for fourteen days) and provide multiple storage solutions.

Maintenance Integration: The best emergency supplies are worthless if they've expired or degraded. We provide detailed rotation schedules and inspection protocols to keep your preparations fresh and functional.

Family-Centered Approach: Every recommendation considers the needs of children, adults, seniors, and pets. Special sections address unique medical needs, mobility considerations, and comfort items that maintain morale during stressful situations.

Community Connection: True resilience extends beyond individual households. We include strategies for neighborhood cooperation, skill sharing, and mutual aid that multiply your preparedness effectiveness.

What Makes This Guide Different

Unlike basic emergency checklists, this guide provides:

- **Specific quantities and calculations** for every recommended item
- **Multiple options** for different budgets and living situations
- **Maintenance schedules** to keep everything current and functional
- **Advanced strategies** that go beyond basic survival to maintain quality of life
- **Integration methods** for working with neighbors and community resources
- **Continuous improvement systems** to adapt and enhance your

INTRODUCTION

preparations over time

Getting Started: Your Preparedness Journey

Emergency preparedness isn't an all-or-nothing proposition. This guide is designed to support gradual building over time, with clear priorities and budget-conscious options. Whether you're starting with a basic 72-hour kit or expanding existing preparations, you'll find practical next steps and realistic timelines.

The most important step is simply getting started. Every gallon of water stored, every flashlight tested, and every plan discussed with your family boosts your resilience and peace of mind. This guide will help you systematically work toward true preparedness. Not just surviving emergencies, but maintaining dignity, comfort, and community no matter what challenges come your way.

Chapter 1

Water & Hydration Systems

"Ensuring a reliable supply of clean drinking water is the foundation of any emergency plan."

Water is essential for life. In emergencies, you can survive weeks without food but only days without water. For a family of four preparing for a 14-day emergency, water storage and purification are your most important readiness efforts. This chapter offers a comprehensive system for storing, purifying, and managing water supplies that will keep your family hydrated and healthy through any crisis.

1.1 Storage Requirements & Calculations

The Basic Formula: One Gallon Per Person Per Day

Emergency preparedness experts universally advise storing one gallon of water per person per day. This covers drinking (half a gallon), cooking (one quart), and basic hygiene (one quart). For a family of four planning a 14-day supply:

Total Water Needed: 4 people × 1 gallon × 14 days = **56 gallons**

This may seem like a massive amount, but we'll break it down into manageable storage solutions that fit most homes and budgets.

CHAPTER 1

Storage Container Options
Large Capacity Barrels (Primary Storage)

- Four 14-gallon water storage barrels with spigots
- Food-grade plastic with UV protection
- Stackable design saves space
- Built-in spigots for easy dispensing
- *Cost: $40-60 per barrel*

Mid-Size Jugs (Portable Backup)

- Two 5-gallon BPA-free water jugs with handles and caps
- Easy to move and transport
- Perfect for vehicle storage
- Can double as washing/cleaning water
- *Cost: $15-25 per jug*

Emergency Transport (Grab-and-Go)

- Two collapsible 5-liter water carriers
- Pack flat when empty
- Essential for evacuation scenarios
- Lightweight and durable
- *Cost: $12-20 each*

Maximum Storage Option (Space Permitting)

- One 55-gallon food-grade drum
- Most cost-effective per gallon
- Requires a pump for water removal
- Best for basements or garages
- *Cost: $80-120 with pump*

Storage Best Practices
Location Requirements

- Cool, dark environment (under 75°F preferred)
- Avoid direct sunlight to prevent algae growth
- Above ground level to prevent freezing
- Away from chemicals, gasoline, or pesticides
- Accessible during emergencies

Container Preparation

1. Sanitize new containers with a mild bleach solution (1 tablespoon per gallon)
2. Rinse thoroughly until no chlorine smell remains
3. Fill with fresh municipal water (already chlorinated)
4. Label with the fill date using a permanent marker
5. Seal tightly and store properly

Space-Saving Solutions

- Stack barrels with plywood between layers
- Use under-stair spaces or closets
- Consider outdoor storage sheds with temperature control
- Rotate locations seasonally if needed

1.2 Purification Methods & Equipment

Even the best storage system needs backup purification methods. Municipal water can become contaminated, stored water can develop issues, and you may need to use questionable sources during extended emergencies.

Chemical Purification
Water Purification Tablets

- 200-tablet pack treats up to 200 liters
- Effective against bacteria, viruses, and some parasites
- Lightweight and shelf-stable for 5 years
- Follow timing instructions precisely (usually 30 minutes)
- *Cost: $15-25 per 200-pack*

Household Bleach Method

- Use unscented household bleach (6-8% sodium hypochlorite)
- Formula: 8 drops per gallon of clear water
- Wait 30 minutes before drinking
- Water should have a slight chlorine smell
- Store bleach in a cool, dark location
- *Cost: $2-4 per gallon of bleach*

Physical Filtration
Personal Filter Straws

- LifeStraw or a similar brand for individual use
- Filters up to 1,000 gallons per unit
- Removes bacteria and parasites instantly
- Perfect for grab-and-go kits
- No batteries or moving parts required
- *Cost: $15-25 each*

Pump Filter Systems

- Katadyn or MSR brand with replaceable cartridges
- Filters 100,000+ liters per cartridge set
- Handles large quantities efficiently
- Works with any water source
- Portable for camping or evacuation
- *Cost: $80-150 with an extra cartridge*

Gravity-Fed Filter Systems

- Berkey or similar stainless-steel system
- No pumping required. Gravity does the work
- Filters 1-6 gallons per hour, depending on model
- Removes bacteria, viruses, chemicals, and heavy metals
- Long-term countertop solution
- *Cost: $200-400, depending on size*

Boiling Equipment
Portable Camp Stoves

- Jetboil or Coleman single-burner system
- Fuel canisters stored safely for years
- Bring water to a rolling boil for 1+ minutes
- Most reliable purification method available
- Works regardless of contamination type
- *Cost: $50-100 plus fuel*

Solar Water Disinfection

- Clear plastic bottles in direct sunlight
- 6 hours of strong sun kills most pathogens
- Backup method requiring no equipment
- Works in warm climates only
- Not effective against chemical contamination

1.3 Alternative Sources & Collection

When stored water runs low, alternative sources become critical. Knowing how to safely collect and process water from various sources multiplies your water security exponentially.

Rainwater Harvesting

CHAPTER 1

Basic Rain Barrel System

- 55-gallon barrel with mesh filter top
- First-flush diverter to avoid roof contaminants
- Downspout diverter kit for easy installation
- Spigot near the bottom for water removal
- *Cost: $60-120 complete system*

Advanced Collection Setup

- Multiple barrels connected in series
- Overflow system to prevent flooding
- Fine mesh filters to remove debris
- Covered storage to prevent mosquito breeding
- Can collect 600+ gallons from 1 inch of rain on an average roof

Safety Considerations

- Always filter and purify collected rainwater
- Avoid the first 10 minutes of rainfall (roof washing)
- Check roof materials for toxicity (avoid lead paint areas)
- Clean gutters regularly if using them for collection

Natural Water Sources
Source Quality Assessment

- Fast-moving streams are preferred over stagnant pools
- Clear water is generally safer than cloudy water
- Avoid areas downstream from roads, farms, or industrial sites
- Look for healthy vegetation as an indicator of clean water
- Always purify regardless of appearance

Collection Techniques

- Collect from the fastest-moving section
- Use clean containers or water bags
- Filter through cloth first to remove large particles
- Allow sediment to settle before treatment
- Boil for 3+ minutes at higher altitudes

Emergency Water Sources in Your Home
Hidden Household Water

- Hot water heater: 40-50 gallons (drain from bottom valve)
- Toilet tank water: 2-5 gallons per toilet (tank only, not bowl)
- Ice maker and refrigerator reservoirs: 1-3 gallons
- Pipes: 2-5 gallons (open highest and lowest faucets)

Pool and Spa Water

- Requires extensive filtration and purification
- Remove chlorine with activated carbon
- Boil after filtering for safety
- Last resort only due to chemical treatment

1.4 Maintenance & Rotation Protocols

The best water storage system is worthless if the water has gone bad or the equipment doesn't work. Regular maintenance keeps your water safe and your equipment functional.

Water Rotation Schedule
Every 6 Months

1. Empty all storage containers completely
2. Inspect containers for cracks, cloudiness, or odors
3. Sanitize with mild bleach solution (1 tablespoon per gallon)
4. Rinse thoroughly until no chlorine smell remains

5. Refill with fresh municipal water
6. Label with new fill date
7. Update your calendar for the next rotation

Monthly Quick Checks

- Visual inspection of all containers
- Check for leaks or damage
- Verify storage area temperature and conditions
- Test one container for taste and odor
- Ensure all spigots and caps work properly

Equipment Maintenance
Filter System Maintenance

- Test filtration rate monthly (should maintain flow)
- Replace cartridges according to manufacturer's schedule
- Clean housing and connections quarterly
- Store spare cartridges in a cool, dry location
- Keep a maintenance log with replacement dates

Purification Supply Management

- Check expiration dates on tablets and chemicals
- Rotate bleach annually (loses potency over time)
- Test equipment functionality quarterly
- Replace batteries in any powered equipment
- Maintain instruction sheets in waterproof storage

Troubleshooting Common Issues
Stored Water Problems

- *Cloudy water*: Usually harmless minerals, but filter and purify

- *Strange taste*: Often from plastic containers, usually safe but off-putting
- *Green tinge*: Algae growth from light exposure, purify before use
- *Bad smell*: Bacterial growth possible, discard and sanitize the container

Equipment Issues

- *Slow filtration*: Clean or replace the filter cartridge
- *Cracked containers*: Patch with food-safe sealant or replace
- *Frozen water*: Thaw slowly, check containers for damage
- *Contaminated source water*: Use multiple purification methods

Creating Your Water Management System
Documentation

- Keep a water journal with fill dates and rotation schedule
- Maintain equipment manuals in waterproof storage
- Post an emergency water location map somewhere the family can see it
- Include water instructions in your family emergency plan

Family Training

- Teach all family members how to operate the equipment
- Practice water collection and purification methods
- Assign specific roles for water management during emergencies
- Conduct quarterly water preparedness drills

Budget-Friendly Implementation

- Start with basic storage: 2-3 weeks of water in smaller containers
- Add purification methods gradually (tablets first, then filters)
- Build storage capacity over 6-12 months
- Look for sales on containers during the camping season

Emergency Water Rationing

If your water supply runs low, implement rationing immediately:
Survival Minimum: 1/2 gallon per person per day

- Drinking: 2-3 quarts
- Food preparation: 1-2 cups
- Hygiene: Minimal, focus on hands and face

Conservation Strategies

- Use paper plates to avoid washing dishes
- Take sponge baths instead of showers
- Collect and reuse gray water for non-drinking purposes
- Prioritize drinking water over cooking water
- Use hand sanitizer instead of soap and water when possible

Chapter Summary: Building Your Water Security Foundation

Water storage and purification form the bedrock of emergency preparedness. By implementing the systems outlined in this chapter, you'll have:

✓ **56 gallons of stored water** for your family's 14-day supply
✓ **Multiple purification methods** for questionable water sources
✓ **Alternative collection systems** to extend your water independence
✓ **Maintenance protocols** to keep everything fresh and functional
✓ **Family training** so everyone knows how to access and manage water

Next Steps: Start with basic storage containers and one purification method. Build your system gradually, testing each component as you add it. Remember, the best water system is one that's maintained regularly and familiar to your entire family.

Now that the water is secured, we'll focus on the next survival priority: building a comprehensive food and nutrition plan that keeps your family well-fed and healthy during long-term emergencies.

Chapter 2

Food & Nutrition Planning

"To feed a family of four for 14 days (fifty-six person-days), you'll need a mix of proteins, complete meals, snacks, plus the tools to prep and rotate everything."

After securing your water supply, food becomes your second survival priority. But emergency food planning goes beyond simply stockpiling calories—you need balanced nutrition, variety to maintain morale, and systems to keep everything fresh and accessible. This chapter transforms food storage from a pantry-stuffing exercise into a strategic nutrition system that keeps your family well-fed and healthy during extended emergencies.

2.1 Non-Perishable Protein Sources

Protein provides essential amino acids, helps maintain muscle mass during stress, and creates satisfying meals that boost morale. Your 14-day emergency food supply should emphasize shelf-stable proteins that require minimal preparation.

Canned Protein Strategy

The Foundation Formula: For optimal nutrition and variety, plan on **two protein servings per person per day** during emergencies. This higher-than-normal protein intake helps maintain strength during physically and emotionally demanding situations.

Tuna (5 oz cans)

- Quantity needed: 56 cans total
- Calculation: one can per person per day × four people × fourteen days
- Benefits: High protein, omega-3 fatty acids, ready-to-eat
- Storage tip: Mix water-packed and oil-packed for variety
- Cost: $1.50-2.50 per can = $85-140 total

Chicken (5 oz cans)

- Quantity needed: 56 cans total
- Provides a variety of alternative to tuna
- Higher protein content than most canned meats
- Works in multiple recipe applications
- Choose low-sodium versions when available
- Cost: $2.00-3.00 per can = $115-170 total

Canned Fish Alternatives

- Salmon: Higher cost but excellent nutrition (12-15 cans)
- Sardines: Compact, calcium-rich, budget-friendly (20-30 small cans)
- Mackerel: High omega-3 content, distinctive flavor (10-15 cans)

Plant-Based Protein Powerhouses
Beans & Legumes (15 oz cans)

- Quantity needed: 56 cans total
- Varieties: Black beans, kidney beans, chickpeas, lentils
- Benefits: Fiber, complex carbohydrates, plant protein
- Recipe versatility: Soups, stews, salads, sides
- Cost: $0.80-1.50 per can = $45-85 total

Protein Combinations for Complete Amino Profiles

- Rice + beans = complete protein equivalent to meat
- Peanut butter + whole grain crackers = balanced nutrition
- Hummus + pita = satisfying, protein-rich meal

Specialty Protein Options
Canned Beef & Pork

- Higher cost but familiar flavors for picky eaters
- Vienna sausages, canned ham, beef stew
- 10-15 cans for variety and comfort food appeal

Nut Butters & Seeds

- Peanut butter: 4 jars (16 oz each) for high-calorie protein
- Almond or sunflower seed butter for nut allergies
- Individual nut packets for portable snacking

2.2 Ready-to-Eat Meal Solutions

Complete meals eliminate guesswork, provide balanced nutrition, and reduce cooking fuel requirements. Building a foundation of ready-to-eat options ensures your family stays well-fed even when cooking isn't possible.

Military Meals Ready-to-Eat (MREs)
Why MREs Excel in Emergencies

- Complete nutritional balance (1,200+ calories per meal)
- 5-year shelf life in proper storage conditions
- Self-heating capability with included flameless ration heaters
- No refrigeration or special storage requirements
- Battle-tested reliability in extreme conditions

MRE Planning

- Quantity needed: 56 meals total
- Calculation: 1 per person per day × 4 people × 14 days
- Variety strategy: Order mixed cases to prevent menu fatigue
- Popular flavors: Beef stew, chicken and rice, vegetable lasagna
- Cost: $8-12 per meal = $450-675 total

MRE Storage & Management

- Store at 70°F or below for maximum shelf life
- Rotate stock using "first in, first out" system
- Check packaging for damage or swelling
- Keep heating elements dry and functional

Freeze-Dried Entrees
Advantages of Freeze-Dried Meals

- Lightweight (important for evacuation scenarios)
- 25 to 30-year shelf life when properly stored
- Retain most original nutritional value
- Quick preparation with hot water only
- Compact storage footprint

Freeze-Dried Planning

- Quantity needed: 56 pouches total
- Requires: 1-2 cups of hot water per serving
- Rehydration time: 8-15 minutes, depending on the meal
- Top brands: Mountain House, Wise Company, Augason Farms
- Cost: $6-10 per serving = $340-560 total

Preparation Requirements

- Reliable water heating method (camp stove, emergency fuel)
- Extra water allocation (beyond drinking/hygiene needs)
- Insulated containers to maintain temperature during rehydration

Commercial Emergency Food Kits
Pre-Packaged Family Kits

- 30-day to 1-year supply options available
- Balanced meal planning done for you
- Often more economical than individual purchases
- Bucket or case storage for easy handling
- Brands: Wise, Legacy, ReadyWise, Mountain House

Kit Evaluation Criteria

- Calorie count per person per day (aim for 1,800+ calories)
- Variety of meals and flavors included
- Preparation requirements (water, heat, equipment)
- Shelf life and storage conditions
- Cost per serving compared to individual items

2.3 High-Energy Snacks & Supplements

Snacks provide psychological comfort, quick energy between meals, and portable nutrition for work or evacuation scenarios. Strategic snacking also helps stretch main meal portions when supplies run low.

Energy-Dense Snack Categories
Granola & Energy Bars

- Quantity needed: 112 bars total
- Calculation: 2 bars per person per day × 4 people × 14 days
- Selection criteria: 200+ calories, 5+ grams protein, minimal sugar
- Varieties: Granola bars, protein bars, meal replacement bars

- Storage: Cool, dry location to prevent melting or staleness
- Cost: $1-2 per bar = $115-225 total

Nuts & Trail Mix

- Quantity needed: 14 lbs total
- Calculation: ¼ lb per person per day (about 2 oz servings twice daily)
- Benefits: Healthy fats, protein, minerals, long-lasting energy
- Varieties: Mixed nuts, trail mix, individual nut types
- Storage tip: Vacuum-sealed packages prevent rancidity
- Cost: $6-10 per lb. = $85-140 total

Dried Fruits & Natural Sugars

- Quantity needed: 7 lbs. total
- Calculation: 1 oz per person per day (about two tablespoons)
- Benefits: Natural sugars, vitamins, fiber, quick energy
- Varieties: Raisins, dried apricots, banana chips, dates
- Avoid: Dried fruits with added sugar or preservatives
- Cost: $4-8 per lb. = $30-55 total

Comfort Food & Morale Boosters
Peanut Butter Power

- Quantity: 4 jars (16 oz each)
- Uses: Sandwiches, snacking, cooking ingredient, calorie booster
- Benefits: 190 calories per 2-tablespoon serving, complete protein when combined with grains
- Storage: Keeps well at room temperature, no refrigeration needed
- Alternative: Almond butter for nut-allergic family members

Sweet Treats for Stress Relief

- Dark chocolate bars (antioxidants + mood boost)
- Honey sticks or packets (natural energy + antimicrobial properties)
- Hard candies (quick sugar + psychological comfort)
- Hot chocolate mix (warming comfort drink)

Salty Snacks & Electrolytes

- Crackers with salt content help maintain electrolyte balance
- Jerky provides protein + sodium for active situations
- Salted nuts replace electrolytes lost through stress sweating

Nutritional Supplements
Multivitamin Insurance

- 60-day supply for each family member
- Compensates for reduced fresh food variety
- Focus on vitamins C, D, and B-complex during stress
- Children's chewable versions for easier compliance

Protein Powder Backup

- 2-3 containers for meal supplementation
- Useful when appetite is low due to stress
- Can boost the calorie content of limited food supplies
- Choose unflavored or vanilla for versatility

Electrolyte Replacements

- Powder packets or tablets for water flavoring
- Essential if experiencing heat stress or physical exertion
- Helps maintain proper hydration with plain water
- More effective than sports drinks for emergency use

2.4 Storage Systems & Inventory Management

The best emergency food is worthless if it's expired, infested, or inaccessible when you need it. Professional storage and inventory management transforms your food stockpile into a reliable nutrition system.

Optimal Storage Conditions
The Storage Triangle: Temperature, Humidity, Light

- **Temperature**: Below 75°F is ideal, avoid temperature fluctuations
- **Humidity**: Below 60% to prevent mold and spoilage
- **Light**: Dark storage prevents nutrient degradation and packaging breakdown

Storage Location Requirements

- Off the floor (use pallets, shelving, or platforms)
- Away from exterior walls where the temperature fluctuates
- Protected from pests (sealed containers, regular inspection)
- Easily accessible during emergencies (no digging through storage)
- Organized by expiration dates for easy rotation

Container & Organization Systems
Food-Grade Storage Containers

- 5-gallon buckets with gamma seal lids for bulk items
- Clear plastic storage bins for easy inventory visibility
- Mylar bags with oxygen absorbers for long-term storage
- Glass jars for smaller quantities and pest protection

Labeling & Dating System

- Label every package with the "Stocked On" date
- Use permanent markers that won't fade over time

- Color-code labels by expiration year for quick identification
- Include contents and serving size on labels

First-In-First-Out (FIFO) Rotation

- Organize shelving so the oldest items are most accessible
- Use older items in regular cooking before they expire
- Replace used items immediately to maintain emergency levels
- Create shopping lists based on upcoming expirations

Inventory Management Tools
Digital Tracking Systems

- Spreadsheet with item, quantity, expiration date, and location
- Smartphone apps for barcode scanning and alerts
- Cloud storage for family member access
- Automated reminders for rotation schedules

Physical Inventory Methods

- Clipboard checklist attached to the storage area
- Monthly walkthrough and count verification
- Visual inspection for damage, pests, or expiration
- Quick-access inventory list posted in the kitchen

Preparation Equipment & Tools
Essential Cooking Tools

- Manual can openers: 2 (store one in each main location)
- Collapsible bowls and utensils: 4 sets for easy cleanup
- Cutting boards: 2 (one for proteins, one for other foods)
- Sharp knives in protective sheaths: 2

Heat Sources for Food Preparation

- Portable camp stove with fuel canisters
- Alternative: Emergency fuel tablets or camping alcohol stove
- Wind screens for outdoor cooking efficiency
- Lighter fluid or waterproof matches for ignition

Food Prep & Storage Accessories

- Resealable plastic bags (quart size): 200-count for portion control
- Heavy-duty aluminum foil: 2 rolls for cooking and food wrapping
- Parchment paper: Prevents sticking, easier cleanup
- Disposable plates and utensils: Reduce water usage for washing

Meal Planning & Recipe Development
14-Day Emergency Menu Planning

- Plan three meals + 2 snacks per person per day
- Rotate protein sources to prevent menu fatigue
- Include one "comfort meal" per week for morale
- Balance hot and cold meal options based on fuel availability

Simple Emergency Recipes

- **Protein + grain + vegetables** = complete meal template
- Tuna and rice with canned vegetables
- Bean and pasta soup with crackers
- Chicken salad with dried fruit and nuts

Water-Conserving Cooking Methods

- One-pot meals minimize cleanup and water needs
- Steam cooking retains nutrients and uses less water

- Cold meal options for when fuel is limited
- Rehydration techniques for dried foods

Budget-Friendly Implementation Strategy
Phase 1: Foundation Building (Month 1-2)

- Focus on canned proteins and basic grains
- Buy sale items in bulk during discount seasons.
- Start with a 7-day supply, then expand
- Cost: $200-300 for basic foundation

Phase 2: Variety & Completion (Month 3-4)

- Add MREs and freeze-dried options
- Include comfort foods and snacks
- Complete 14-day supply for all categories
- Cost: $300-500 additional investment

Phase 3: Optimization & Backup (Month 5-6)

- Add redundant supplies for high-use items
- Include specialty diet items if needed
- Create evacuation-portable food kits
- Cost: $150-250 for optimization

Special Dietary Considerations
Food Allergies & Intolerances

- Gluten-free: Rice-based meals, certified GF products
- Nut allergies: Seed butters, careful label reading
- Dairy-free: Plant-based proteins, coconut milk alternatives
- Multiple restrictions: Focus on single-ingredient whole foods

Medical Diet Requirements

- Diabetic: Low-glycemic options, portion control packets
- Low sodium: Rinse canned items, choose "no salt added" versions
- Renal diet: Limit protein, phosphorus, and potassium as prescribed
- Soft foods: For elderly family members or dental issues

Troubleshooting Common Food Storage Problems
Pest Prevention & Management

- Bay leaves in storage containers deter insects
- Diatomaceous earth around storage areas (food grade only)
- Regular inspection and immediate isolation of affected items
- Professional pest control if the problem persists

Expired Food Assessment

- Canned goods are often safe 1-2 years past the "best by" date if properly stored
- Check for rust, dents, or swelling before use
- Trust your senses: if it looks, smells, or tastes off, discard
- When in doubt, throw it out—food poisoning during an emergency is dangerous

Storage Container Failures

- Backup containers are ready for immediate transfer
- Regular inspection prevents surprise failures
- Quality containers are worth the investment for long-term storage
- Multiple smaller containers are better than a single large failure point

Chapter Summary: Building Your Family's Food Security

A well-planned emergency food system provides more than just calories—

it maintains nutrition, morale, and family stability during challenging times. By implementing the strategies in this chapter, you'll have:

✓ **Balanced protein sources** from both animal and plant origins
✓ **Complete meal solutions** requiring minimal preparation
✓ **Energy-dense snacks** for sustained nutrition and comfort
✓ **Professional storage systems** keep everything fresh and accessible
✓ **Inventory management,** ensuring nothing expires or goes to waste
✓ **Preparation capability** to create satisfying meals under any conditions

Implementation Priority Order:

1. Start with canned proteins and basic starches
2. Add ready-to-eat meals for convenience
3. Include high-energy snacks and comfort foods
4. Develop storage and rotation systems
5. Practice cooking with emergency equipment

With water and food security established, we'll address the third critical element of family safety: comprehensive medical preparedness and first aid systems that keep your family healthy when professional medical care isn't available.

Chapter 3

Medical & First Aid Preparedness

"Ensuring your family can treat injuries, manage chronic conditions, and address sudden illnesses is critical when professional medical care isn't available."

Medical emergencies don't wait for convenient times, and disasters often disrupt access to hospitals, pharmacies, and emergency services. A comprehensive medical preparedness system enables your family to handle everything from minor cuts to serious injuries, manage chronic conditions without pharmacy access, and maintain health during extended emergencies. This chapter transforms basic first aid into a complete family healthcare system.

3.1 Comprehensive First Aid Kits

A well-designed first aid kit goes beyond simple bandages to cover a wide range of injuries and medical situations your family might face. Using professional-grade supplies and proper training can save lives when help is not immediately available.

Core First Aid Foundation

Wound Care & Bleeding Control: Your main goal is to stop bleeding and prevent infection. These are the two leading causes of preventable death in emergencies.

Bandages & Dressings (Quantities for Family of Four)

- Adhesive bandages (assorted sizes): 50-count
- Mix: 30 standard strips, 15 knuckle/fingertip, five large patches
- Quality matters: fabric bandages stay on better than plastic ones.
- Cost: $15-25 for a quality variety pack
- Sterile gauze pads: 50 total
- 25 × 2"×2" pads for small wounds
- 25 × 4"×4" pads for larger injuries
- Individual sterile packaging prevents contamination
- Cost: $20-30 for medical-grade sterile pads
- Non-stick sterile pads: 10-count
- Prevents dressing from adhering to wounds
- Essential for burns and abrasions
- Teflon or petroleum-coated surfaces
- Cost: $10-15 for quality non-stick pads
- Roller gauze (medical tape alternative):
- 2 rolls × 2" width, 2 rolls × 3" width
- Secures dressings without tape residue
- Conforms to body contours better than tape
- Cost: $8-12 for medical-grade elastic gauze

Elastic Support & Immobilization

- ACE bandages: 2 large (4"), 2 medium (3")
- Sprains, strains, and joint support
- Compression for swelling control
- Reusable with proper care
- Cost: $6-10 each for quality elastic bandages

Advanced Wound Management

- Trauma shears (scissors): 1 pair
- Cuts through clothing, seat belts, thick materials
- Angled design prevents accidental skin cuts
- Stainless steel for sterilization capability
- Cost: $15-25 for medical-grade trauma shears
- Fine-point tweezers: 1 precision pair
- Splinter removal and foreign object extraction
- Stainless steel with non-slip grip
- Sharp points for accurate control
- Cost: $8-15 for surgical-grade tweezers

Antiseptic & Infection Prevention
Chemical Antiseptics

- Antiseptic wipes: 50-count
- Alcohol-based for equipment sterilization
- Individual packaging prevents drying out
- Essential for cleaning hands before treatment
- Cost: $8-12 for medical-grade wipes
- Antibacterial ointment: 4 tubes (1 oz each)
- Triple antibiotic (bacitracin, neomycin, polymyxin)
- Prevents infection in minor wounds
- One tube per family member plus backup
- Cost: $12-18 for name-brand antibiotics
- Hydrogen peroxide: 4 oz bottle
- Wound irrigation and cleaning
- Foaming action removes debris
- Also useful for equipment sterilization
- Cost: $3-5 for pharmacy-grade solution
- Alcohol prep pads: 50-count
- Individual sterile packaging
- Equipment sterilization and skin preparation
- Compact and lightweight for portable kits

- Cost: $5-8 for medical-grade prep pads

Emergency Response Tools
Assessment & Monitoring Equipment

- Digital thermometer: 1 with extra batteries
- Fever detection and infection monitoring
- Hypothermia assessment in cold emergencies
- Battery-powered for reliability
- Cost: $10-20 for a medical-grade digital thermometer
- Instant cold packs: 4-count
- Immediate cold therapy for injuries
- No refrigeration required
- Single-use activation by crushing
- Cost: $2-4 each for pharmaceutical-grade packs
- CPR face shield: 2-count
- Barrier protection during rescue breathing
- One-way valve prevents contamination
- Compact pocket-sized storage
- Cost: $5-10 each for medical training quality

Specialized Treatment Supplies
Burn & Thermal Injury Care

- Burn gel packets: 6-count
- Immediate cooling and pain relief
- Sterile application prevents infection
- Individual packets prevent cross-contamination
- Cost: $3-5 per packet for medical-grade gel
- Emergency space blankets: 4-count
- Hypothermia prevention and shock treatment
- Reflects 90% of body heat when properly applied
- Compact, lightweight, and waterproof

- Cost: $2-4 each for emergency medical quality

Fracture & Sprain Management

- Finger splints (assorted sizes): 4-count
- Immediate stabilization of finger injuries
- Aluminum with foam padding for comfort
- Adjustable to fit various finger sizes
- Cost: $8-15 for a medical splint set
- Triangular bandages: 4-count
- Arm slings and large wound dressings
- Immobilization of shoulder and arm injuries
- Multiple uses beyond traditional sling application
- Cost: $10-15 for sterile medical-grade bandages

Storage & Organization
Medical Container Requirements

- Weatherproof, durable container (tackle box or medical bag style)
- Clear compartments for easy inventory and access
- A latching lid that won't open accidentally
- Carrying handle for portability during emergencies
- Cost: $25-50 for professional medical storage

Organization Best Practices

- Group supplies by function (wound care, medications, tools)
- Label compartments with contents and expiration dates
- Keep instruction cards with each supply category
- Include family medical information and emergency contacts
- Attach the inventory checklist to the inside lid

3.2 Prescription Medication Management

Prescription medications become critical lifelines during emergencies when pharmacies are closed or unreachable. Strategic medication management ensures the continuous treatment of chronic conditions and prevents medical emergencies from becoming life-threatening situations.

Medication Inventory & Planning

14-Day Supply Strategy The standard emergency recommendation of 3-7 days of medications is inadequate for most disaster scenarios. Build toward a 14-day minimum supply with backup documentation.

Essential Documentation for Each Medication

- Complete prescription information (medication name, dosage, frequency)
- Prescribing physician contact information
- Pharmacy details and prescription numbers
- Insurance information for emergency refills
- Medical condition being treated and criticality level

High-Priority Medications (Life-Dependent)

- Heart medications (blood pressure, rhythm, anticoagulants)
- Diabetes medications (insulin, metformin, glucose control)
- Respiratory medications (inhalers, nebulizer treatments)
- Seizure control medications (cannot be stopped abruptly)
- Mental health medications (antidepressants, anti-anxiety, mood stabilizers)

Insulin & Diabetes Management

Insulin Storage & Backup Systems

- 14-day supply plus 25% buffer (approximately 18 days total)
- Insulin cooling case for power outage situations

- Battery-powered mini-refrigerator for extended cooling
- Ice packs and insulated storage as backup cooling
- Cost: $50-150 for a complete cooling backup system

Blood Glucose Monitoring

- Extra glucose meter with backup batteries
- Test strips: 14-day supply plus 50% buffer (approximately 150 strips)
- Lancets: 100-count for finger stick testing
- Glucose tablets for hypoglycemia treatment
- Ketone testing strips for diabetic emergency assessment

Emergency Glucose Management

- Glucagon emergency injection kit (prescription required)
- Fast-acting glucose sources (tablets, gel, candy)
- Complex carbohydrate sources for sustained glucose control
- Emergency carbohydrate counting reference cards

Respiratory Medication Systems
Inhaler Management & Backup

- Primary inhaler plus one backup for each family member
- Spacer devices for more effective medication delivery
- Peak flow meter for asthma monitoring
- Nebulizer with extra medication vials if prescribed
- Battery backup for electric nebulizer systems

Allergy & Anaphylaxis Prevention

- EpiPens: 2 per person with severe allergies
- Check expiration dates quarterly (18-month typical lifespan)
- Training for all family members on proper EpiPen use

- Medical alert bracelets for severe allergy identification
- Antihistamine backup (Benadryl) for mild reactions

Medication Storage & Rotation
Optimal Storage Conditions

- Temperature control: Most medications are stable at 68-77°F
- Humidity control: Below 60% to prevent degradation
- Light protection: Dark storage prevents photodegradation
- Air exposure: Keep medications in original containers with desiccant packets

Rotation Management System

- First-in-first-out rotation using the oldest medications first
- Monthly expiration date checking with calendar reminders
- Pharmacy coordination for early refill allowances
- Insurance pre-authorization for emergency supplies
- Documentation system tracking all medication changes

Emergency Prescription Access

- Maintain relationships with multiple pharmacy locations
- Keep prescription copies in the emergency document kit
- Research 24-hour pharmacy locations in your area
- Understand insurance emergency refill policies
- Consider mail-order pharmacy backup relationships

3.3 Over-the-Counter Medicine Cabinet

A well-stocked OTC medicine cabinet handles common ailments that become more serious without treatment. Strategic selection covers the most likely health issues while avoiding redundancy and waste.

Pain & Inflammation Management

Multi-Modal Pain Relief Strategy Different medications work through different pathways, allowing safer and more effective pain control when used appropriately.

Ibuprofen (Anti-Inflammatory)

- Quantity: 200 tablets × 200mg strength
- Uses: Inflammation, fever, muscle pain, headaches
- Advantages: Reduces swelling and inflammation
- Cautions: Avoid with kidney disease, blood thinners, stomach ulcers
- Cost: $8-15 for generic 200-count bottles

Acetaminophen (Fever Reducer)

- Quantity: 200 tablets × 500mg strength
- Uses: Pain relief, fever reduction
- Advantages: Safe with most other medications, gentle on the stomach
- Cautions: Liver damage with excessive use or alcohol consumption
- Cost: $8-15 for generic 200-count bottles

Topical Pain Relief

- Aspercreme or similar topical analgesic (2 tubes)
- Provides localized pain relief without systemic medication
- Useful for muscle strains, arthritis, and minor injuries
- Cost: $6-12 per tube for name-brand topicals

Digestive & Gastrointestinal Support

Diarrhea Control

- Loperamide (Imodium): 50 caplets
- Essential for preventing dehydration during stomach illness
- Particularly important when water supplies are limited

- It can be lifesaving in severe gastroenteritis situations
- Cost: $8-12 for generic 50-count packages

Antacid & Stomach Protection

- Calcium carbonate tablets: 100-count
- Treats heartburn, acid indigestion, and calcium deficiency
- Chewable form for faster action and easier administration
- Safe for most people, including pregnant women
- Cost: $5-10 for generic 100-count bottles

Nausea & Motion Sickness

- Dramamine or meclizine: 50 tablets
- Critical for evacuation travel and stress-related nausea
- Non-drowsy formulations available for daytime use
- Cost: $8-15 for motion sickness relief

Respiratory & Allergy Relief
Antihistamine Coverage

- Diphenhydramine (Benadryl): 100 capsules
- Allergic reactions, insect bites, mild anaphylaxis
- Sedating effect can help with sleep during stress
- Injectable form available for severe reactions
- Cost: $8-12 for generic 100-count bottles

Decongestant Support

- Pseudoephedrine: 50 tablets (requires ID purchase)
- Effective nasal decongestion for sinus pressure
- Helps prevent secondary sinus infections
- Cost: $10-15 for pharmacy-regulated quantities

Cough Suppression

- Dextromethorphan cough syrup: 2 bottles
- Suppresses dry, unproductive coughs
- Helps maintain sleep during respiratory illness
- Available in liquid and tablet forms
- Cost: $8-12 per bottle for generic formulations

Specialized Treatments
Eye & Vision Care

- Lubricating eye drops: 4 bottles
- Artificial tears for dry eyes, dust, and smoke irritation
- Antihistamine eye drops for allergic reactions
- Saline solution for eye irrigation and contact lens care
- Cost: $15-25 for a complete eye care kit

Topical Skin Treatments

- Hydrocortisone cream (1%): 2 tubes
- Anti-itch treatment for rashes, insect bites, and minor skin irritation
- Safe for most skin conditions and age groups
- Cost: $5-10 per tube for pharmacy-grade cream

Cold & Flu Combination

- Multi-symptom cold medication: 2 packages
- Covers multiple symptoms with a single medication
- Day/night formulations for symptom-appropriate treatment
- Cost: $12-18 for name-brand combination packages

Dosage & Safety Management
Family Dosage Charts

- Create laminated reference cards with age-appropriate dosing
- Include weight-based dosing for children
- Note medication interactions and contraindications
- Post in the medicine storage area for emergency reference

Medication Safety Protocols

- Never exceed recommended doses without medical guidance
- Check expiration dates before use (replace annually)
- Read all labels for active ingredients to avoid duplication
- Keep medications in original containers with dosing instructions
- **Maintain poison control contact information (1-800-222-1222)**

3.4 Special Medical Needs Planning

Every family has unique medical requirements that go beyond standard first aid. Comprehensive medical preparedness addresses individual health needs, age-specific requirements, and medical equipment dependencies that become critical during emergencies.

Age-Specific Medical Planning

Infant & Child Specialties Children aren't small adults—they require different medications, dosing, and medical approaches during emergencies.

Pediatric Medication Adjustments

- Children's ibuprofen (100mL): Age-appropriate pain and fever relief
- Acetaminophen suppositories (20 count): For vomiting children who can't keep oral medication down
- Oral rehydration salts: Pediatric formulation for diarrhea/vomiting
- Thermometer probe covers (20 count): Sanitary temperature monitoring
- Cost: $25-40 for a complete pediatric medication kit

Infant-Specific Emergency Supplies

- Bulb syringe: Nasal congestion relief and airway clearing
- Infant acetaminophen drops: Precise dosing for the youngest children
- Diaper rash cream: Prevents skin breakdown during hygiene challenges
- Teething gel: Pain relief during the natural development process
- Cost: $15-25 for infant-specific medical supplies

Senior & Mobility Considerations Older adults face unique challenges during emergencies, from medication management to mobility limitations.

Enhanced Prescription Management

- Pill organizers: Weekly compartment systems for multiple medications
- Pill crusher: For patients with swallowing difficulties
- Large-print medication labels and dosing instructions
- Backup mobility aids: Extra cane tips, walker glides, crutch padding
- Cost: $20-35 for a senior medication management system

Vision & Hearing Support

- Extra eyeglasses with current prescriptions
- Magnifying glass for reading medication labels
- Hearing aid batteries (20 count) with battery tester
- Amplified telephone or communication board for the hearing impaired
- Cost: $30-50 for vision and hearing backup supplies

Chronic Medical Condition Support
Cardiovascular Disease Management

- Blood pressure monitoring cuff with backup batteries
- Heart rate monitor for exercise and stress monitoring
- Low-sodium diet planning cards and reference materials
- Compression stockings for circulation support during limited mobility
- Cost: $40-80 for cardiovascular monitoring equipment

Respiratory Disease Support

- Peak flow meter for asthma monitoring and medication timing
- Portable oxygen concentrator battery backup (if prescribed)
- Air quality monitor for smoke, dust, and allergen detection
- Nebulizer cleaning and sterilization supplies
- Cost: $60-120 for respiratory support equipment

Diabetes Advanced Management

- Continuous glucose monitor backup supplies
- Insulin pen needles (100 count) for injection systems
- Glucose gel packets for rapid hypoglycemia treatment
- Diabetic emergency identification cards for first responders
- Cost: $40-70 for advanced diabetes emergency support

Medical Equipment & Power Backup
CPAP & Sleep Apnea Equipment

- Battery backup power system (8 to 12-hour capacity)
- Extra CPAP filters and cleaning supplies
- Manual resuscitation mask as emergency backup
- Sleep positioning aids for non-CPAP sleep management
- Cost: $200-400 for a complete CPAP backup system

Oxygen & Respiratory Support

- Portable oxygen concentrator with battery backup
- Extra nasal cannulas and tubing (sterile packaging)
- Pulse oximeter for oxygen level monitoring
- Manual ventilation bag for emergency respiratory support
- Cost: $300-800 for oxygen support backup system

Emergency Medical Information Systems
Medical Alert & Identification

- Medical alert bracelets or necklaces for each family member with conditions
- Emergency medical information cards in wallets and vehicles
- Refrigerator emergency medical information sheet for first responders
- Digital medical information storage on encrypted USB drives
- Cost: $25-50 for a complete medical identification system

Healthcare Provider Communication

- Primary care physician contact information
- Specialist contact information (cardiologist, endocrinologist, etc.)
- Hospital preference and insurance information
- Medication allergy and adverse reaction documentation
- Cost: Primarily organizational time investment

Emergency Medical Decision Documentation

- Healthcare power of attorney documents
- Living will and advance directive copies
- DNR orders if applicable (keep originals accessible)
- Organ donation preferences and documentation
- Cost: Legal consultation $200-500 for comprehensive healthcare directives

Training & Family Preparedness
Medical Training Priorities

- CPR certification for all capable family members
- First aid certification through the Red Cross or a similar organization
- Basic life support training, including AED use

- Family-specific medical training (insulin injection, inhaler use, etc.)
- Cost: $100-200 per person for comprehensive medical training

Practice & Skill Maintenance

- Monthly medical drill scenarios with different family members as patients
- Quarterly equipment checks and battery replacements
- Annual recertification for CPR and first aid skills
- Family medical emergency plan review and updates
- Cost: Ongoing time investment with periodic recertification fees

Chapter Summary: Building Your Family's Medical Resilience

Comprehensive medical preparedness goes far beyond basic first aid to create a complete healthcare system that maintains family health when professional medical care isn't available. By implementing the strategies in this chapter, you'll have:

✓ **Professional-grade first aid capabilities** for treating injuries from minor to serious

✓ **Prescription medication management,** ensuring continuous treatment of chronic conditions

✓ **Complete over-the-counter pharmacy** addressing common ailments before they become serious

✓ **Age and condition-specific planning** meeting every family member's unique medical needs

✓ **Medical equipment backup systems** maintain critical health support during power outages

✓ **Emergency medical documentation** enabling proper treatment by first responders

✓ **Family medical training** creates multiple people capable of providing emergency care

Implementation Priority Order:

1. Build a comprehensive first aid kit with professional-grade supplies
2. Secure a 14-day supply of all prescription medications
3. Stock strategic over-the-counter medications for common conditions
4. Address special needs and age-specific requirements
5. Create medical documentation and communication systems
6. Obtain medical training for all capable family members

Budget-Friendly Implementation:

- Start with prescription medications (most critical for chronic conditions)
- Build a first aid kit gradually, focusing on wound care first
- Add OTC medications during pharmacy sales and with store coupons
- Seek group discounts for family medical training classes
- Total investment: $300-600 for complete family medical preparedness

With your family's immediate survival needs secured through water, food, and medical preparedness, we'll move to the tools and equipment that enable you to maintain, repair, and fortify your home during extended emergencies.

Chapter 4

Tools, Repair & Maintenance

"Equipping your household with the right tools and materials ensures you can repair damage, reinforce your home, and perform essential maintenance during an emergency."

When disaster strikes, your ability to repair damage, maintain critical systems, and adapt your environment can mean the difference between comfort and crisis. Professional-grade tools and strategic repair materials transform you from helpless victim to capable problem-solver. This chapter builds a comprehensive repair and maintenance system that handles everything from basic fixes to major damage control.

4.1 Essential Hand Tools Collection

The right tools form the foundation for all repair work, maintenance tasks, and emergency modifications. Quality tools work reliably under stress and last for decades when properly cared for.

Core Tool Categories

Multi-Function Tools (Always Accessible) Every family member should carry or have immediate access to a quality multi-tool for daily needs and emergency situations.

Primary Multi-Tool

- Leatherman Wave+ or similar professional-grade multi-tool
- Features: Pliers, wire cutters, knife, saw, scissors, awl, rulers
- Stainless steel construction with replaceable components
- Belt holster for immediate accessibility
- Cost: $80-120 for a professional-grade multi-tool

Fixed-Blade Backup Knife

- 4 to 6-inch bushcraft or utility knife with full tang construction
- Uses: Heavy cutting, prying, food preparation, self-defense
- Carbon steel holds a better edge than stainless steel for heavy use
- Leather sheath for safe storage and belt carry
- Cost: $40-80 for a quality bushcraft knife

Folding Pocket Knives

- Two high-quality folding knives (one per adult)
- 3 to 4-inch blades with locking mechanisms
- Everyday carry for countless daily tasks
- Backup tools when a multi-tool isn't available
- Cost: $25-50 each for reliable folding knives

Cutting & Shaping Tools
Hand Saws for Various Materials
Different materials require different saw types—having the right saw makes difficult jobs manageable.
Handsaw (Wood Cutting)

- 20 to 24-inch crosscut saw with aggressive teeth
- Cuts dimensional lumber, plywood, and tree branches
- Essential for structural repairs and modifications
- Hardened steel teeth maintain sharpness longer
- Cost: $25-40 for a professional carpenter's saw

Folding Saw (Portability)

- Compact folding design for storage and transport
- Aggressive tooth pattern cuts green wood and seasoned lumber
- Locks open for safety during use
- Fits in toolbox or emergency kit
- Cost: $20-35 for a quality folding saw

Hacksaw with Extra Blades

- Metal cutting capability for pipes, bolts, and hardware
- Include 10 extra blades (different teeth per inch for various materials)
- Adjustable frame accommodates different blade lengths
- Essential for plumbing and mechanical repairs
- Cost: $15-25 for a hacksaw plus $10-15 for blade assortment

Striking & Prying Tools
Claw Hammer (16 oz)

- Balanced weight for extended use without fatigue
- Curved claw for nail removal and prying
- Steel or fiberglass handle for durability
- Most versatile striking tool for general repairs
- Cost: $25-40 for a professional-grade hammer

Pry Bar/Crowbar (24-30 inch)

- Heavy-duty steel construction with multiple pry points
- Demolition, debris removal, and forced entry capability
- Flat end for prying, pointed end for precise work
- Essential for storm damage cleanup
- Cost: $20-35 for a professional pry bar

Dead Blow Hammer

- Sand-filled head prevents bounce and tool damage
- Precise striking without marring surfaces
- Useful for assembly work and delicate adjustments
- Reduces user fatigue during extended use
- Cost: $20-30 for a quality dead blow hammer

Fastening & Assembly Tools
Screwdriver Set (Complete) A comprehensive screwdriver set handles the vast majority of fastener types encountered in repairs.
Flat Head Screwdrivers

- Sizes: 1/8", 3/16", 1/4", 5/16", 3/8" blade widths
- Various lengths for different access requirements
- Magnetic tips help hold screws during installation
- Insulated handles for electrical work safety
- Cost: $30-50 for complete professional set

Phillips Head Screwdrivers

- Sizes: #0, #1, #2, #3, #4 Phillips points
- #2 Phillips most commonly used size
- Stubby versions for tight spaces
- Magnetic tips prevent dropped screws
- Cost: $25-40 for a complete Phillips set

Specialty Screwdrivers

- Torx set for modern fasteners (T10, T15, T20, T25, T30)
- Robertson (square drive) for Canadian-made items
- Precision set for electronics and small appliances
- Cost: $20-35 for specialty screwdriver assortment

Adjustable Wrenches

- Small (6-8 inch): Tight spaces and smaller fasteners
- Medium (10-12 inch): General purpose, most common size
- Wide jaw opening accommodates various bolt sizes
- Non-slip grip handles for better torque application
- Cost: $15-25 each for quality adjustable wrenches

Gripping & Holding Tools

Pliers Set (Professional Grade) Different plier types handle specific gripping and manipulation tasks that fingers cannot manage.

Slip-Joint Pliers

- 8 to 10 inch length with adjustable jaw positions
- General-purpose gripping, twisting, and pulling
- Insulated handles for electrical safety
- Wire cutting capability in most designs
- Cost: $15-25 for professional slip-joint pliers

Needle-Nose Pliers

- Long, narrow jaws reach into tight spaces
- Precision gripping of small objects
- Wire bending and electrical connector work
- Side cutting edges for wire trimming
- Cost: $12-20 for quality needle-nose pliers

Locking Pliers (Vice-Grips)

- Adjustable jaw with locking mechanism
- Hands-free clamping and holding capability
- Emergency tool for damaged bolt heads
- Multiple jaw configurations available

- Cost: $15-25 for the original Irwin Vice-Grip brand

Measuring & Marking Tools
Tape Measure (25-foot)

- Heavy-duty case with belt clip
- Magnetic tip adheres to metal surfaces
- Clear markings in both standard and metric
- Standout capability for measuring without assistance
- Cost: $15-25 for a professional-grade tape measure

Combination Square

- 90-degree and 45-degree angle measurements
- Precise marking for cuts and layout work
- Built-in level for horizontal and vertical alignment
- Scribing capability for marking measurements
- Cost: $20-35 for machinist-quality square

Chalk Line

- 100-foot chalk line for long, straight marking
- Essential for large construction and repair projects
- Refillable chalk reservoir with various color options
- Self-retracting line with automatic rewinding
- Cost: $12-20 for a professional chalk line reel

4.2 Fasteners & Repair Materials

Having the right fasteners and repair materials immediately available prevents delays and enables immediate repairs. Strategic stockpiling covers the most common repair scenarios without excessive inventory.

Nail & Screw Assortments

Nail Selection Strategy Different nail types serve specific purposes—having variety enables proper fastening for each application.

Common Nails (5 lbs. total)

- 1-inch: Light trim work, thin materials
- 1.5-inch: Standard trim, light framing
- 2-inch: Medium framing, plywood attachment
- 2.5-inch: Heavy framing, structural repairs
- 3-inch: Thick materials, strong joints
- Cost: $15-25 for a 5-lb assorted nail selection

Finishing Nails (2 lbs. total)

- Small heads sink below the surface for a clean appearance
- Sizes: 1", 1.5", 2", 2.5" lengths
- Interior trim work and visible fastening
- Galvanized coating prevents rust
- Cost: $12-18 for a 2-lb finishing nail assortment

Roofing Nails (3 lbs.)

- Large heads prevent material pull-through
- Galvanized coating for weather resistance
- 1.5" length for standard roofing applications
- Essential for emergency roof repairs
- Cost: $8-12 for a 3-lb roofing nail supply

Screw Selection for Maximum Versatility

Wood Screws (500 pieces total)

- Lengths: 1/2", 1", 1.5", 2", 2.5", 3" (mixed assortment)
- Phillips head for universal compatibility
- Self-tapping points eliminate pilot holes in soft materials

- Zinc coating prevents corrosion
- Cost: $25-40 for a 500-piece wood screw assortment

Metal Screws (200 pieces)

- Self-tapping screws for sheet metal work
- Hex head or Phillips head options
- Various lengths from 1/2" to 2"
- Essential for HVAC, ducting, and metal repairs
- Cost: $15-25 for a metal screw variety pack

Masonry Screws (50 pieces)

- Tapcon or similar brand concrete screws
- Drill into concrete, brick, or block without anchors
- Include appropriate masonry drill bits
- Essential for securing items to concrete foundations
- Cost: $20-30 for a masonry screw kit with bits

Bolts, Nuts & Heavy-Duty Fasteners
Hex Bolt Assortment (200 sets)

- Sizes: 1/4", 5/16", 3/8", 1/2" diameters
- Lengths: 1", 1.5", 2", 2.5", 3" for each diameter
- Include matching nuts and washers for each bolt
- Grade 5 steel for high-strength applications
- Cost: $40-60 for complete bolt, nut, washer assortment

Carriage Bolts (50 pieces)

- Square neck prevents bolt rotation during tightening
- Smooth, rounded heads for safety and appearance
- Common sizes: 1/4" × 2", 5/16" × 2.5", 3/8" × 3"

- Include wing nuts for tool-free adjustment
- Cost: $15-25 for carriage bolt assortment

Flexible Fastening Systems

Zip Ties (200 pieces total) Modern repairs increasingly rely on flexible fastening systems that accommodate movement and vibration.

Small Zip Ties (4-inch, 100 pieces)

- Cable management and small item securing
- UV-resistant nylon construction
- 18-lb tensile strength for light-duty applications
- Black color for inconspicuous installations
- Cost: $8-12 for a 100-piece small zip tie pack

Medium Zip Ties (8-inch, 75 pieces)

- General-purpose bundling and securing
- 40-lb tensile strength for moderate loads
- Weather-resistant for outdoor applications
- Most versatile size for emergency repairs
- Cost: $10-15 for a 75-piece medium zip tie pack

Large Zip Ties (12-inch, 25 pieces)

- Heavy-duty securing and temporary structural support
- 75-lb tensile strength for demanding applications
- Extra width distributes the load over a larger area
- Emergency repairs requiring significant holding power
- Cost: $8-12 for a 25-piece heavy-duty zip tie pack

Tape Solutions for Every Situation

Duct Tape (6 rolls)

- 60-yard rolls of professional-grade duct tape
- Waterproof, flexible, and adheres to most surfaces
- Emergency repairs, weatherproofing, bundling
- Silver color is the most versatile, including colored rolls for coding
- Cost: $5-8 per roll for quality duct tape

Electrical Tape (4 rolls)

- Insulating tape for electrical repairs and marking
- Various colors for wire identification and phasing
- Flame-retardant and moisture-resistant
- Essential for electrical system emergency repairs
- Cost: $3-5 per roll for professional electrical tape

Paracord & Rope Solutions
Paracord 550 (200 feet)

- Seven-strand construction with 550-lb test strength
- Multiple uses: securing, bundling, emergency rope
- Inner strands are removed for lighter-duty applications
- Compact storage, high strength-to-weight ratio
- Cost: $15-25 for 200 feet of military-spec paracord

Bungee Cords (8 pieces, assorted sizes)

- Elastic cords with hooks for temporary securing
- Sizes: 12", 18", 24", 36" lengths
- UV-resistant rubber withstands outdoor exposure
- Quick-release securing without permanent installation
- Cost: $12-20 for an assorted bungee cord set

Adhesives & Sealants
Wood Glue (2 bottles, waterproof)

- Titebond III or similar waterproof wood adhesive
- Stronger than the wood itself when properly applied
- Essential for furniture repairs and woodworking projects
- An 8-hour working time allows complex assemblies
- Cost: $8-12 per bottle for professional wood glue

Epoxy Resin (2-part kit)

- Quick-setting epoxy for emergency repairs
- Bonds dissimilar materials: metal, plastic, ceramic, wood
- Waterproof cure suitable for outdoor applications
- Gap-filling capability for imperfect joints
- Cost: $10-15 for a professional two-part epoxy kit

Construction Adhesive (2 tubes)

- Heavy-duty adhesive for large surface bonding
- Subfloor repairs, panel installation, and weatherproofing
- Flexible cure accommodates building movement
- Weather-resistant for exterior applications
- Cost: $6-10 per tube for construction-grade adhesive

4.3 Vehicle Maintenance Capabilities

Vehicle reliability becomes critical during emergencies when professional repair services may be unavailable. Basic vehicle maintenance capability keeps your family mobile and maintains your primary evacuation asset.

Emergency Roadside Repair Kit
Jump Starting & Electrical

- Heavy-duty jumper cables (20 feet, 4-gauge wire)
- Portable jump starter battery pack (lithium-ion preferred)
- Electrical multimeter for diagnostic work

- Electrical repair kit: wire, connectors, fuses
- Cost: $100-150 for a complete electrical emergency kit

Tire Repair & Inflation

- Tire repair kit with plugs and patches
- Portable tire inflator (12V or battery-powered)
- Tire pressure gauge (accurate to ±1 PSI)
- Emergency tire sealant for temporary repairs
- Cost: $60-100 for tire emergency repair system

Fluid Management

- Motor oil (2 quarts, appropriate viscosity for your vehicle)
- Coolant/antifreeze (1 gallon, 50/50 pre-mixed)
- Power steering fluid (1 quart)
- Brake fluid (1 pint, DOT 3 or 4 as specified)
- Cost: $30-50 for vehicle fluid emergency supply

Basic Automotive Tools
Socket Set (Metric & Standard)

- 1/4" drive set for small fasteners and tight spaces
- 3/8" drive set for general automotive work
- 1/2" drive set for larger fasteners and high-torque applications
- Include extension bars and universal joints
- Cost: $60-120 for a complete automotive socket set

Automotive Wrenches

- Combination wrench set (8mm-19mm metric, 5/16"-3/4" standard)
- Adjustable wrenches (8" and 12" sizes)
- Oil filter wrench for routine maintenance

- Spark plug socket with rubber insert
- Cost: $40-80 for automotive wrench collection

Specialized Automotive Tools

- Battery terminal cleaner and protector
- Funnel set for fluid changes and additions
- Work light (LED, magnetic base, rechargeable)
- Mechanic's stethoscope for engine diagnostics
- Cost: $35-60 for specialized automotive tools

Vehicle Towing & Recovery
Tow Strap System

- Heavy-duty tow strap (20 feet, rated for 2× vehicle weight)
- Tow hooks or D-rings for attachment points
- Safety chains as a backup to the primary tow connection
- Warning flags for extended equipment visibility
- Cost: $40-80 for a complete vehicle recovery system

Come-Along Winch

- Manual cable winch (2-ton capacity minimum)
- 20 feet of steel cable with hooks
- Tree protection straps to prevent bark damage
- Used for vehicle extraction from ditches or obstacles
- Cost: $60-120 for a manual winch recovery system

4.4 Home Fortification Supplies

Securing and reinforcing your home turns it from a vulnerable shelter into a defensible stronghold. Strategic fortification materials allow for quick responses to different threat levels.

Window & Door Security

Window Protection Systems Windows represent the most vulnerable points in home security—proper protection dramatically improves overall security.

Plywood Boarding Materials

- 4×8 foot plywood sheets (1/2" thickness): 4 sheets
- Pre-cut to fit major windows for rapid deployment
- Drill pilot holes and number each sheet for quick identification
- Weather-resistant exterior-grade plywood
- Cost: $35-50 per sheet for exterior-grade plywood

Security Window Film

- 4 mil security film (rolls to cover major windows)
- Holds glass together if broken, and prevents easy entry
- UV protection prevents interior fading
- Professional appearance maintains home aesthetics
- Cost: $2-4 per square foot for security window film

Window Security Bars (Removable)

- Adjustable bars that fit standard window frames
- Quick-release mechanisms for emergency egress
- Powder-coated steel construction
- Visible deterrent effect on potential intruders
- Cost: $25-50 per window for adjustable security bars

Door Reinforcement Systems
Door Frame Strengthening

- Door jamb reinforcement plates (steel, four pieces)
- 3-inch security screws for door frame attachment

- Strike plate reinforcement with extended strike boxes
- Align reinforcement with door deadbolt locations
- Cost: $15-25 per door for frame reinforcement kit

Additional Door Security

- Heavy-duty deadbolts (Grade 1 ANSI rating)
- Door security bars (floor-to-door bracing systems)
- Sliding door security bars and locks
- Chain locks and door viewers for controlled access
- Cost: $40-80 per door for a complete security upgrade

Perimeter Security Materials
Fencing & Barrier Materials

- Chain link fencing sections (portable, interlocking)
- Fence posts and mounting hardware
- Privacy screening for visual concealment
- Gate hardware and locking mechanisms
- Cost: $15-25 per linear foot for temporary fencing

Lighting & Surveillance Support

- Motion-sensor flood lights (solar or battery-powered)
- Outdoor extension cords (heavy-duty, weather-resistant)
- Security camera mounting brackets and hardware
- Timer switches for automated lighting patterns
- Cost: $30-60 per light fixture installed

Emergency Shelter Reinforcement
Structural Repair Materials

- 2×4 lumber (8 feet): 20 pieces for emergency bracing

- Construction screws (3-inch): 5 lbs for structural attachment
- Metal brackets and braces for joint reinforcement
- Plastic sheeting (6 mil) for weather protection
- Cost: $100-150 for emergency structural repair supplies

Weatherproofing & Sealing

- Roofing tar and patch materials for leak repairs
- Caulking compounds for gap sealing
- Weather stripping for door and window sealing
- Vapor barrier plastic for moisture control
- Cost: $50-100 for complete weatherproofing supplies

Tool Storage & Organization
Secure Tool Storage

- Heavy-duty tool chest with locking mechanisms
- Weather-resistant storage for outdoor tool security
- Organization systems prevent loss and enable quick access
- Inventory control prevents tool "migration"
- Cost: $150-400 for a professional tool storage system

Portable Tool Organization

- Tool rolls for hand tool transport
- Bucket organizers for portable tool collections
- Magnetic tool holders for metal surface organization
- Label systems for quick identification and inventory
- Cost: $30-80 for portable tool organization system

Maintenance & Inventory Management
Tool Maintenance Supplies

- Multi-purpose lubricant (WD-40 type): 2 cans
- Cutting oil for drilling and threading operations
- Sharpening stones for blade maintenance
- Cleaning rags and brushes for tool care
- Cost: $20-35 for tool maintenance supplies

Inventory & Documentation

- Tool inventory checklist with purchase dates
- Maintenance log for tool sharpening and repairs
- Instruction manuals in waterproof storage
- Parts lists and supplier contact information
- Cost: Primarily organizational time investment

Chapter Summary: Building Your Repair & Maintenance Capability

A comprehensive tool and repair system transforms your family from helpless disaster victims into capable problem-solvers who can maintain, repair, and fortify their environment under any conditions. By implementing the systems in this chapter, you'll have:

✓ **Professional-grade hand tools** capable of handling any repair or modification task

✓ **Strategic fastener inventory** enabling immediate repairs without store trips

✓ **Vehicle maintenance capability,** keeping your primary transportation reliable

✓ **Home fortification materials** transforming your house into a secure stronghold

✓ **Organization systems** keep everything accessible and inventory current

✓ **Maintenance protocols** ensuring tools remain sharp, functional, and reliable

Implementation Priority Order:

1. Acquire a core hand tool collection (multi-tool, hammer, screwdrivers, wrenches)
2. Build fastener inventory focusing on the most common sizes and types
3. Establish vehicle emergency repair capability
4. Add home fortification and security materials
5. Create organization and storage systems
6. Develop maintenance routines and inventory management

Budget-Friendly Implementation Strategy:

- **Phase 1** (Months 1-2): Core hand tools and basic fasteners ($200-300)
- **Phase 2** (Months 3-4): Vehicle tools and repair materials ($150-250)
- **Phase 3** (Months 5-6): Home fortification and specialized tools ($200-400)
- **Total Investment**: $550-950 for complete repair and maintenance capability

Quality vs. Cost Considerations:

- Buy quality hand tools once rather than cheap tools repeatedly
- Generic fasteners perform as well as name brands at a lower cost
- Vehicle-specific tools are worth the investment for reliability
- Home fortification materials: functionality over appearance

Storage Space Requirements:

- Minimum: One dedicated closet or large cabinet
- Optimal: Workshop area or garage with workbench
- Vehicle storage: Emergency kit fits in sedan trunk
- Consider climate control for tool longevity

With home repair and maintenance capabilities established, we'll focus on power, lighting, and communication systems that keep your family connected and functional when the electrical grid fails.

Chapter 5

Lighting, Power & Communications

"Keeping your household illuminated, devices charged, and lines of communication open is critical when the grid goes down."

When the power grid fails, your family faces an immediate triple threat: darkness, dead devices, and a communication blackout. Professional lighting, power, and communication systems restore normalcy, maintain safety, and keep your family connected to the outside world. This chapter builds integrated systems that provide reliable illumination, sustainable power, and multiple communication pathways regardless of grid status.

5.1 Portable Lighting Solutions

Strategic lighting extends beyond basic visibility to create psychological comfort, facilitate productive work, and ensure security during prolonged power outages. A layered lighting approach provides the right illumination for every situation and need.

Personal Lighting Systems

Individual Flashlights (One Per Person) Every family member needs immediate access to reliable personal lighting that doesn't depend on shared resources.

High-Output LED Flashlights

- Quantity: 4 tactical-grade LED flashlights (one per person)
- Specifications: 800+ lumen output, multiple brightness levels
- Battery: AA or 18650 rechargeable lithium-ion preferred
- Features: Strobe mode for signaling and tail switch for tactical operation
- Runtime: 8+ hours on low setting, 2+ hours on high setting
- Cost: $40-80 each for quality tactical flashlights

Hands-Free Headlamps

- Quantity: 4 LED headlamps for hands-free operation
- Applications: Repair work, cooking, reading, navigation
- Features: Red light mode preserves night vision, adjustable beam focus
- Battery: AAA or rechargeable preferred for weight reduction
- Comfort: Padded headband for extended wear during long tasks
- Cost: $25-50 each for comfortable, reliable headlamps

Backup Lighting Components

- Extra LED bulbs: 8-count (compatible with flashlight models)
- Replacement O-rings: 4 sets for water seal maintenance
- Lens protection: Clear protective covers prevent scratching
- Holsters/clips: Belt and pocket carry options for accessibility
- Cost: $20-40 for a complete backup component kit

Area Lighting Solutions

Battery-Powered Lanterns Area lighting creates comfortable spaces and enables group activities during power outages.

LED Area Lanterns

- Quantity: 2 high-capacity LED lanterns for room illumination

- Specifications: 360-degree light distribution, 600+ lumen output
- Battery: D-cell or rechargeable battery pack options
- Features: Dimmer control, hanging hooks, stable base design
- Runtime: 25+ hours on low setting, 8+ hours on high setting
- Cost: $30-60 each for quality LED area lanterns

Solar & Hand-Crank Lanterns

- Quantity: 2 alternative-powered lanterns for sustainable lighting
- Power sources: Solar panel, hand crank, battery backup combination
- Advantages: No battery replacement needed, environmentally sustainable
- Features: Emergency radio integration, USB charging ports for devices
- Applications: Long-term power outages, outdoor use, evacuation scenarios
- Cost: $25-50 each for multi-powered emergency lanterns

Traditional Backup Lighting

Candle Systems (Controlled Environments) candles offer reliable backup lighting without relying on batteries, but they demand careful safety management.

Unscented Pillar Candles

- Quantity: 24 pillar candles (4 to 6 inches in height, 3-inch diameter)
- Burn time: 40-60 hours per candle, depending on size
- Safety: Unscented reduces respiratory irritation in enclosed spaces
- Storage: Cool, dry location prevents warping and wick deterioration
- Cost: $3-6 per candle for quality long-burning pillars

Hurricane Lanterns

- Quantity: 4 traditional hurricane-style lanterns with glass chimneys
- Fuel: Lamp oil or liquid paraffin (cleaner burning than kerosene)

- Safety: Glass chimney protects flame from wind and reduces fire risk
- Light output: Equivalent to a 40-watt incandescent bulb per lantern
- Cost: $15-30 each for quality hurricane lanterns plus fuel

Candle Safety Equipment

- Snuffers: 4-count for safe flame extinguishing
- Drip plates: 8 count to protect surfaces from wax damage
- Lighter fluid: Wind-resistant ignition for outdoor use
- Matches: Waterproof strike-anywhere matches (5 boxes)
- Cost: $15-25 for complete candle safety accessories

Emergency Signaling Lights
High-Visibility Signaling

- Glow sticks: 20 medium-intensity sticks (6-hour duration each)
- Signal mirror: 1 military-grade signaling mirror
- Flare alternatives: LED emergency beacons with strobe capability
- Reflective markers: Tape and panels for marking safe areas
- Cost: $25-40 for a complete emergency signaling kit

5.2 Power Generation & Storage

Sustainable power systems provide the electrical foundation for lighting, communications, medical equipment, and device charging. Multiple power sources ensure redundancy when primary systems fail.

Battery Power Management

Primary Battery Inventory: Strategic battery stockpiling covers all family devices with appropriate reserves for extended outages.

Alkaline Battery Stock

- AA batteries: 100 alkaline + 16 rechargeable NiMH
- AAA batteries: 100 alkaline + 16 rechargeable NiMH

- C batteries: 20 alkaline (radio and lantern power)
- D batteries: 20 alkaline (high-drain lantern applications)
- 9-volt batteries: 10 alkaline (smoke detectors, radios, meters)
- Cost: $80-120 for a complete alkaline battery inventory

Rechargeable Battery System

- Battery charger: Multi-chemistry charger (NiMH, Li-ion compatibility)
- AA rechargeable: 16 high-capacity NiMH (2500+ mAh rating)
- AAA rechargeable: 16 high-capacity NiMH (1000+ mAh rating)
- Charging cycles: Quality NiMH batteries support 500+ charge cycles
- Cost: $60-100 for a complete rechargeable battery system

Portable Power Stations

High-Capacity Power Banks Modern power banks provide substantial device charging capability with multiple output options.

Individual Power Banks

- Quantity: 4 high-capacity units (20,000+ mAh each)
- Features: Multiple USB ports, USB-C PD, wireless charging capability
- Device compatibility: Smartphones, tablets, small electronics
- Charging cycles: 300+ full charge cycles before capacity degradation
- Cost: $40-80 each for quality 20,000+ mAh power banks

Family Power Station

- Capacity: 100-200 Wh portable battery station
- Outputs: AC outlets, 12V DC, multiple USB ports
- Applications: CPAP machines, small appliances, device charging
- Charging: AC wall charging, 12V car charging, solar panel input
- Cost: $200-500 for mid-capacity portable power station

Solar Power Systems

Portable Solar Charging Solar power provides sustainable electricity generation independent of fuel supplies or grid connections.

Foldable Solar Panels

- Quantity: 2 panels (15-25 watts each)
- Features: Weatherproof construction, integrated charge controllers
- Compatibility: Direct device charging, power bank charging
- Portability: Foldable design for compact storage and transport
- Cost: $60-120 each for quality portable solar panels

Solar Generator System

- Capacity: 100-500 Wh battery with integrated solar charging
- Components: Battery pack, charge controller, AC/DC outputs
- Applications: Emergency power for essential devices and lighting
- Expandability: Additional solar panels for faster charging
- Cost: $300-800 for a complete solar generator system

Alternative Power Generation

Hand-Crank & Dynamo Power Mechanical power generation provides electricity independent of weather, fuel, or battery condition.

Hand-Crank Radio/Flashlight Combos

- Quantity: 2 combination units for redundancy
- Power generation: 1-2 minutes of cranking provides 10-15 minutes of operation
- Features: AM/FM/NOAA radio, LED flashlight, USB device charging
- Advantages: No battery dependency, unlimited operational capability
- Cost: $25-50 each for quality hand-crank emergency radios

Pedal-Power Generator (Advanced Option)

- Type: Bicycle generator or exercise bike conversion

- Output: 50-100 watts sustained power generation
- Applications: Device charging, lighting, small appliance operation
- Exercise benefit: Maintains physical fitness during sedentary emergency periods
- Cost: $200-500 for pedal-powered generator system

Backup Generator Options

Portable Gas Generators. For families with adequate outdoor space and fuel storage capability, portable generators provide substantial power capacity.

Mid-Size Portable Generator

- Power output: 2,000-3,000 watts continuous power
- Runtime: 8-12 hours on a 5-gallon fuel tank
- Features: Multiple outlets, 12V DC charging, electric start preferred
- Applications: Refrigerator, heating/cooling, power tools, device charging
- Cost: $400-800 for a quality portable generator

Generator Support Equipment

- Fuel storage: 2 × 5-gallon DOT-approved gas cans
- Fuel stabilizer: Treats 20 gallons of gasoline for long-term storage
- Extension cords: Heavy-duty outdoor-rated cords (25-50 feet)
- Transfer switch: Safe connection to home electrical panel
- Cost: $150-300 for generator support equipment

Generator Safety Requirements

- Carbon monoxide detectors: Battery-powered for generator operation areas
- Ventilation: Minimum 20 feet from windows, doors, vents
- Ground fault protection: GFCI outlets for wet weather operation

- Maintenance schedule: Oil changes, air filter replacement, fuel rotation
- Cost: $50-100 for generator safety equipment

5.3 Communication Equipment

Communication systems maintain family coordination, provide emergency information, and enable contact with outside resources. Multiple communication methods ensure connectivity when primary systems fail.

Weather & Emergency Information

NOAA Weather Radio Systems Official weather information and emergency alerts provide critical decision-making information during disasters.

Battery-Powered NOAA Radios

- Quantity: 2 dedicated weather radios for redundancy
- Features: All-hazard alert capability, SAME technology for local alerts
- Power: Battery operation plus AC adapter and hand-crank backup
- Coverage: Monitors all 7 NOAA weather frequencies automatically
- Cost: $30-60 each for quality NOAA weather radios

Weather Radio Features & Setup

- Alert programming: Set for local county codes and hazard types
- Battery backup: Maintain fresh batteries for power-outage operation
- Antenna positioning: External antenna improves reception in difficult areas
- Volume control: Adjustable alerts prevent sleep disruption for minor alerts
- Testing: Weekly test of alert functions and battery condition

Two-Way Radio Communications

Family Coordination Radios Two-way radios enable family coordination, work party communication, and neighborhood networking when

cellular systems fail.
Mid-Range Walkie-Talkies

- Quantity: 4 handheld radios (one per family member)
- Range: 1-2 miles in suburban terrain, longer in open areas
- Features: Multiple channels, privacy codes, VOX hands-free capability
- Battery: Rechargeable battery packs plus AA battery backup capability
- Cost: $40-80 each for quality FRS/GMRS handheld radios

Two-Way Radio Accessories

- Extra battery packs: 4 rechargeable lithium-ion battery packs
- Charging station: Multi-unit charging dock for simultaneous charging
- Belt clips: Hands-free carrying for active work situations
- Headsets: Hands-free operation with push-to-talk buttons
- Cost: $60-120 for a complete two-way radio accessory kit

Radio Communication Protocols

- Channel assignment: Designate primary and backup communication channels
- Check-in schedules: Regular status updates during emergency operations
- Code words: Simple codes for common situations and status reports
- Range testing: Verify the communication range from home to key locations
- Documentation: Laminated reference cards with frequencies and procedures

Long-Range Communication

Citizens Band (CB) Radio: CB radio provides long-range communication capability and access to trucking/emergency networks.

Mobile CB Radio System

- Base unit: 40-channel CB radio with weather alert capability
- Antenna: External antenna system for maximum range and clarity
- Installation: Mobile or base station setup with appropriate power supply
- Range: 5-15 miles, depending on terrain and atmospheric conditions
- Cost: $100-200 for a complete CB radio communication system

Amateur Radio (HAM) Considerations

- Licensing: FCC license required for legal amateur radio operation
- Capability: Local, regional, and international communication potential
- Emergency networks: Access to organized emergency communication networks
- Training: Local amateur radio clubs provide licensing and training support
- Cost: $150-500 for entry-level amateur radio equipment

Mobile Device Support

Smartphone & Tablet Charging Mobile devices provide access to information, communication, and navigation when cellular networks remain operational.

Device Charging Solutions

- Car chargers: 12V chargers for vehicle power system use
- Solar chargers: Compact solar panels designed for mobile device charging
- Battery banks: High-capacity external batteries for multiple device charges
- Charging cables: Multiple cable types (Lightning, USB-C, Micro-USB)
- Cost: $50-100 for a complete mobile device charging system

Communication Apps & Preparation

- Offline maps: Download regional maps for GPS navigation without data
- Emergency apps: Red Cross Emergency, FEMA, and local emergency management apps
- Mesh networking: Apps like Bridgefy enable phone-to-phone communication
- Information storage: Emergency contacts, documents, procedures stored locally
- Preparation: Configure apps and download content before emergencies occur

Signaling & Backup Communication
Emergency Signaling Devices

- Whistles: High-decibel safety whistles (4 count, one per person)
- Signal mirror: Military-grade signaling mirror for daylight signaling
- Air horn: Compressed air horn for long-distance audio signaling
- Emergency beacons: Personal locator beacons (PLBs) for extreme emergencies
- Cost: $40-100 for a complete emergency signaling kit

5.4 Power & Communication Integration

Integrated systems maximize efficiency, reduce redundancy, and ensure critical communications remain powered throughout extended emergencies.

Power Priority Management
Essential Device Hierarchy: Strategic power allocation ensures critical devices remain operational when power is limited.

Priority 1: Life Safety

- Medical devices (CPAP, nebulizers, glucose monitors)
- Communication radios (weather alerts, emergency coordination)

- Flashlights and area lighting for safe movement
- Smoke and carbon monoxide detectors

Priority 2: Information & Coordination

- Smartphones for emergency communication and information
- Weather radios for ongoing situational awareness
- Two-way radios for family and neighborhood coordination
- Tablet computers for information access and entertainment

Priority 3: Comfort & Morale

- Larger lighting systems for normal activities
- Entertainment devices for psychological well-being
- Convenience charging for secondary devices
- Non-essential electronic equipment

Power Distribution Systems
Charging Station Setup

- Central charging location with multiple power sources
- Power strips with surge protection for device safety
- The organization system prevents cable confusion and device loss
- Inventory tracking ensures all devices remain charged and accounted
- Cost: $50-100 for an organized central charging station

Load Management

- Power consumption monitoring to prevent system overload
- Scheduled charging rotations when power capacity is limited
- Device power-off protocols to extend battery life
- Alternative power source rotation to prevent single-point failures

Communication Network Design
Family Communication Plan

- Primary communication method: Two-way radios for local coordination
- Backup communication: Cell phones when network capacity allows
- Emergency communication: Signaling devices when electronic systems fail
- Information gathering: Weather radio for official emergency information

Extended Network Integration

- Neighborhood communication: Common radio channels and check-in schedules
- Emergency services: Knowledge of local emergency frequencies and protocols
- Information sharing: Protocols for sharing critical information with neighbors
- Mutual aid coordination: Communication systems supporting community cooperation

Maintenance & Testing Protocols
Equipment Testing Schedule

- Weekly: Battery levels, charging systems, communication device functionality
- Monthly: Power generation systems, solar panel performance, fuel supplies
- Quarterly: Complete system testing, equipment rotation, and inventory updates
- Annually: Equipment replacement, technology upgrades, procedure review

Documentation & Training

- Equipment manuals: Waterproof storage of all instruction manuals
- Operating procedures: Laminated reference cards for emergency use
- Family training: Regular practice with all communication and power systems
- Contact information: Updated emergency contact lists and frequency references

Chapter Summary: Building Your Power & Communication Independence

Reliable lighting, sustainable power, and multiple communication systems provide the technological foundation that maintains family safety, coordination, and morale during extended emergencies. By implementing the systems in this chapter, you'll have:

✓ **Comprehensive lighting solutions** from personal flashlights to area illumination systems

✓ **Sustainable power generation** through batteries, solar, and alternative power sources

✓ **Multi-layered communication capability** for information, coordination, and emergency contact

✓ **Integrated power management** ensuring critical systems remain operational

✓ **Backup and redundancy systems** preventing single points of failure

✓ **Maintenance protocols** keeping all systems functional and ready for use

Implementation Priority Order:

1. Personal lighting (flashlights and headlamps for each family member)
2. Battery inventory and charging systems for immediate power needs
3. Weather radio and basic communication systems for information
4. Area lighting and power bank systems for comfort and device charging
5. Solar power and alternative generation for extended independence

6. Advanced communication systems and network integration

Budget-Friendly Implementation Strategy:

- **Phase 1** (Month 1): Personal lighting and basic batteries ($150-250)
- **Phase 2** (Month 2): Power banks and weather radio ($200-300)
- **Phase 3** (Month 3): Area lighting and two-way radios ($200-350)
- **Phase 4** (Month 4-6): Solar systems and advanced power options ($400-800)
- **Total Investment**: $950-1,700 for complete power and communication independence

System Integration Benefits:

- Reduced battery inventory through standardization on common sizes
- Multiple charging methods prevent power system failures
- Communication redundancy ensures connectivity under various conditions
- Scalable systems support both short-term outages and extended grid failures

Power Consumption Planning:

- Calculate total power needs for essential devices
- Size battery and generation systems for 14-day independence
- Plan power rationing protocols for extended outages
- Identify non-essential devices that can be powered down to conserve energy

Communication Network Advantages:

- Family coordination during separated emergency operations
- Access to official emergency information and weather alerts

- Neighborhood networking capability for mutual aid and information sharing
- Multiple communication pathways prevent isolation during crisis situations

With power and communication systems meeting your technological needs, we'll concentrate on shelter and heating systems that ensure physical comfort and safety in any weather or housing situation.

Chapter 6

Chapter 6: Shelter & Warmth Management

"Creating a safe, insulated space and keeping everyone warm are vital during emergencies when heating systems fail or evacuation becomes necessary."

Shelter and warmth form the cornerstone of survival, providing protection from the elements and maintaining core body temperature that keeps your family alive and functional. Whether you're weathering a power outage at home, establishing a temporary shelter after structural damage, or evacuating to an unknown location, comprehensive shelter and warmth systems ensure your family's physical safety and psychological comfort. This chapter builds layered protection systems that work in any environment or emergency scenario.

6.1 Temporary Shelter Solutions

When your primary residence becomes uninhabitable or evacuation becomes necessary, temporary shelter systems provide immediate protection while maintaining family unity and essential gear security.

Emergency Shelter Systems

Primary Family Tent A quality family tent serves as temporary housing, secure storage, and psychological refuge during displacement emergencies.

Four-Person All-Weather Tent

- Capacity: 4-person with gear storage vestibule
- Construction: Double-wall design with waterproof rainfly (3,000mm+ rating)
- Seasonality: 3-season minimum, 4-season preferred for extreme weather
- Setup: Color-coded poles and clips for quick setup in stress situations
- Durability: Ripstop nylon with reinforced stress points and heavy-duty zippers
- Cost: $200-400 for a quality family emergency shelter tent

Tent Specifications & Features

- Floor space: 60+ square feet for family sleeping with gear
- Peak height: 6 feet minimum for comfortable interior movement
- Ventilation: Multiple vents prevent condensation and maintain air quality
- Access: Two doors prevent bottlenecks during emergency exit situations
- Guy-out points: Storm-rated tie-down points for high-wind stability

Shelter Support Systems

Ground Protection & Insulation Proper ground management prevents moisture infiltration and provides insulation from cold surfaces.

Ground Cloth System

- Footprint tarp: Cut to tent floor dimensions, prevents ground moisture
- Heavy-duty tarp: 10×12 feet for multi-use weather protection
- Grommets: Reinforced attachment points every 2 feet for secure tie-down
- Material: 6-mil polyethylene minimum, vinyl preferred for durability
- Cost: $25-50 for a complete ground protection system

Structural Support Materials

- Tent stakes: 24 heavy-duty aluminum or steel stakes
- Guyline: 100 feet of reflective paracord for visibility and strength
- Mallet: Dead-blow hammer for stake driving without tent damage
- Repair kit: Fabric patches, seam sealer, zipper repair supplies
- Cost: $40-80 for complete tent support and repair system

Multi-Use Tarp Systems

Emergency Weather Protection Tarps provide versatile weather protection that adapts to changing needs and multiple shelter configurations.

Heavy-Duty Tarp Collection

- Large tarp: 12×16 feet for maximum coverage and versatility
- Medium tarp: 8×10 feet for standard family shelter applications
- Small tarp: 6×8 feet for personal shelter or gear protection
- Material: Canvas or vinyl-coated polyester for tear resistance
- Cost: $30-60 each, depending on size and material quality

Tarp Rigging & Support

- Telescoping poles: 4 adjustable poles (6-10 feet) for tarp support
- Bungee cords: 12 heavy-duty cords for quick, adjustable attachment
- Carabiners: 8 aluminum clips for secure rope-to-anchor connections
- Rope: 200 feet of 1/4-inch polyester rope for guy-lines and tie-downs
- Cost: $60-100 for a complete tarp rigging system

Shelter Site Selection & Preparation
Site Assessment Criteria

- Drainage: Avoid low areas where water collects during storms
- Wind protection: Natural or artificial windbreaks reduce heat loss
- Ground conditions: Level, well-drained soil without rocks or roots

- Safety: Distance from hazards like dead trees, power lines, flood zones
- Resources: Proximity to water sources while maintaining a safe distance

Site Preparation Tools

- Folding shovel: An Entrenching tool for drainage and ground leveling
- Rake: Collapsible camp rake for debris removal and ground preparation
- Hand saw: Folding saw for clearing brush and cutting tent stakes
- Work gloves: Heavy-duty gloves for safe handling of debris and materials
- Cost: $40-80 for shelter site preparation tools

6.2 Sleeping & Comfort Systems

Quality sleep and rest restore physical and mental resilience during high-stress emergencies. Professional sleeping systems maintain comfort and warmth regardless of ground conditions or ambient temperature.

Sleep System Foundation

Sleeping Bags (Temperature-Rated) Proper sleeping bags provide the primary thermal barrier that prevents hypothermia and ensures restorative sleep.

Family Sleeping Bag Collection

- Adult bags: 2 sleeping bags rated to 10°F below local winter lows
- Child bags: 2 sleeping bags appropriate for smaller body sizes
- Bag type: Mummy bags for maximum warmth, rectangular for comfort preference
- Fill: Synthetic insulation for wet-weather performance and easy care
- Cost: $80-150 each for quality cold-weather sleeping bags

Sleeping Bag Features & Selection

- Temperature ratings: Use the EN/ISO rating system for accurate

comparisons
- Zipper compatibility: Left and right zip bags can connect for couples
- Compression stuff sacks: Reduce packed size for transportation
- Draft collars: Prevent warm air loss around the neck and shoulders
- Hood design: Adjustable hood systems retain head warmth efficiently

Ground Insulation Systems

Sleeping Pads (Critical for Warmth) Ground insulation prevents body heat loss to cold surfaces—often more important than sleeping bag quality.

Insulated Sleeping Pads

- Quantity: 4 self-inflating pads with R-value 4.0+ for cold-weather use
- Size: Regular length (72") adequate for most adults, long (78") for taller individuals
- Width: 20-25 inches provides an adequate sleeping surface with efficient packing
- Valve system: Reliable inflation/deflation valves that won't fail in cold weather
- Cost: $60-120 each for quality self-inflating insulated sleeping pads

Backup Ground Insulation

- Closed-cell foam pads: 4 lightweight backup pads that can't puncture or deflate
- Emergency space blankets: 4 reflective blankets for additional ground barrier
- Yoga mats: Multipurpose padding that doubles as exercise and comfort surfaces
- Carpet samples: Free insulation material from flooring stores for ground covering
- Cost: $40-80 for a complete backup insulation system

Comfort & Support Items

Pillow & Head Support Systems

- Inflatable pillows: 4 compact pillows that pack small but provide real comfort
- Pillowcases: 4 washable cotton cases for hygiene and comfort
- Stuff sack pillows: Use clothing-filled stuff sacks as a backup pillow system
- Neck support: Travel pillows for sitting rest and vehicle sleeping
- Cost: $30-60 for a complete family pillow system

Sleep Comfort Enhancements

- Eye masks: 4 sleep masks for daytime rest and light management
- Earplugs: Multiple pairs for noise reduction in chaotic environments
- Essential oils: Lavender or chamomile for stress reduction and sleep aid
- Personal comfort items: Small, familiar objects that aid psychological comfort
- Cost: $25-50 for sleep enhancement accessories

6.3 Climate-Appropriate Clothing Systems

Strategic clothing systems provide adjustable insulation that adapts to changing weather conditions and activity levels. Layering principles enable precise temperature control while maintaining mobility and functionality.

Layering System Principles

Base Layer (Moisture Management) Base layers move sweat away from skin to prevent cooling through evaporation while maintaining warmth.

Moisture-Wicking Base Layers

- Adult tops: 2 long-sleeve merino wool or synthetic base layer shirts per adult
- Adult bottoms: 2 base layer pants/long underwear per adult

- Child layers: 2 complete base layer sets per child (sized appropriately)
- Material preference: Merino wool for odor resistance, synthetic for durability
- Cost: $40-80 per complete base layer set

Base Layer Features & Care

- Seamless construction: Reduces chafing during extended wear
- Antimicrobial treatment: Reduces odor buildup when washing isn't possible
- Quick-dry capability: Enables washing and rapid drying for hygiene
- Fit: Snug but not restrictive, allows full range of motion

Insulation Layer (Warmth Retention)

Mid-Layer Insulation Systems: Mid-layers trap warm air while allowing moisture vapor to pass through to outer layers.

Fleece & Insulated Jackets

- Adult jackets: 2 mid-weight fleece or synthetic insulation jackets per adult
- Child jackets: 2 appropriately-sized insulation layers per child
- Vest options: Sleeveless insulation maintains core warmth with arm mobility
- Zip systems: Full-zip design allows precise temperature regulation
- Cost: $50-100 per mid-layer insulation piece

Insulation Material Comparison

- Fleece: Inexpensive, quick-drying, maintains warmth when wet
- Down insulation: Highest warmth-to-weight ratio, compresses well, loses insulation when wet
- Synthetic fill: Maintains warmth when wet, bulkier than down, more affordable

- Wool: Natural insulation, fire-resistant, maintains warmth when wet

Outer Layer (Weather Protection)

Shell Layer Systems Outer layers provide wind and water protection while allowing moisture vapor to escape from inner layers.

Waterproof-Breathable Shells

- Adult shells: 2 jacket and pant sets per adult with full weather protection
- Child shells: 2 complete weather protection sets sized for children
- Features: Sealed seams, storm flaps, adjustable cuffs, and hem
- Breathability: Gore-Tex or equivalent technology prevents interior condensation
- Cost: $100-250 per complete adult shell system

Shell Layer Features

- Pit zips: Ventilation zippers prevent overheating during active periods
- Storm hoods: Helmet-compatible hoods with adjustable closures
- Reinforcements: Extra material at high-wear areas (knees, seat, shoulders)
- Pocket systems: Secure storage for essential items in weather conditions

Extremity Protection

Hand & Foot Warmth Systems

Extremities lose heat rapidly and require specialized protection to maintain dexterity and circulation.

Hand Protection Layers

- Liner gloves: 4 pairs of thin gloves that maintain dexterity for detailed work
- Insulated gloves: 4 pairs of warm gloves for general outdoor work and weather protection
- Shell mittens: 4 pairs of waterproof outer mittens for maximum warmth

in extreme conditions
- Hand warmers: 20 pairs of disposable chemical hand warmers for emergency warmth
- Cost: $60-120 for a complete family hand protection system

Foot Protection & Warmth

- Waterproof boots: 1 pair per person, insulated and sized for thick socks
- Sock systems: 10 pairs of wool or synthetic socks per person (various thicknesses)
- Boot warmers: Disposable foot warmers for extreme cold conditions
- Gaiters: Leg protection that prevents snow and debris from entering boots
- Cost: $100-200 per person for a complete foot protection system

Clothing Storage & Organization
Clothing Pack Systems

- Compression sacks: Reduce clothing volume for efficient packing
- Waterproof stuff sacks: Protect clothing from moisture during storage/transport
- Organization system: Color-coding or labeling for quick identification
- Spare clothing cache: Additional clothing set stored separately from primary supplies
- Cost: $40-80 for clothing organization and storage system

6.4 Heating & Insulation Methods

Active heating systems and strategic insulation maintain comfortable temperatures and prevent hypothermia when building heating systems fail or shelters lack integrated heating.

Portable Heating Systems
Safe Indoor Heating Options. Indoor heating requires careful attention

to carbon monoxide production and fire safety.

Propane Heaters (Indoor-Safe)

- Heater type: Catalytic or infrared propane heater with oxygen depletion sensor
- Capacity: 4,000-9,000 BTU output appropriate for tent or small room heating
- Fuel: 4 propane canisters (16.4 oz each) provide 32-48 hours total runtime
- Safety features: Automatic shut-off, tip-over protection, low-oxygen cutoff
- Cost: $100-200 for an indoor-safe propane heater with fuel supply

Propane Heater Safety Requirements

- Ventilation: Always provide fresh air exchange to prevent carbon monoxide buildup
- Carbon monoxide detector: Battery-powered CO detector required during heater operation
- Fire extinguisher: ABC-rated extinguisher within reach during heater use
- Clearances: Maintain manufacturer-specified distances from combustible materials
- Never use outdoor-only heaters indoors: Risk of carbon monoxide poisoning

Alternative Heating Methods
Body Heat & Thermal Mass Systems

Passive heating methods require no fuel and provide safe, sustainable warmth.

Body Heat Multiplication

- Buddy system: Share sleeping bags or blankets to combine body heat

- Exercise routines: Calisthenics and movement generate internal heat
- Hot water bottles: Fill bottles with heated water for localized warmth
- Heated stones: Warm rocks by fire, wrap in cloth for a safe heat source
- Cost: Minimal cost for materials, primarily technique-based

Thermal Mass Heating

- Water jugs: Large water containers absorb heat during the day, release it at night
- Sand/dirt bags: Heat-absorbing mass that stores and releases thermal energy
- Concrete blocks: Masonry materials store significant heat energy
- Metal containers: Steel or aluminum containers efficiently conduct and radiate heat
- Cost: $20-50 for thermal mass heating materials

Insulation & Heat Retention
Structural Insulation Improvements: Strategic insulation prevents heat loss and reduces heating fuel requirements.
Reflective Insulation Systems

- Reflective foam panels: 8 sheets of foil-faced foam for wall and floor insulation
- Emergency space blankets: Reflective barriers that redirect body heat
- Reflective window film: Prevents heat loss through glass surfaces
- Radiant barriers: Reflect heat back into living spaces rather than losing it to walls
- Cost: $60-120 for a reflective insulation system

Traditional Insulation Materials

- Fiberglass batts: Temporary insulation for damaged walls or missing insulation

- Foam board: Rigid insulation panels for structural gaps and improvements
- Weather stripping: Seal gaps around doors and windows to prevent drafts
- Plastic sheeting: Temporary vapor barriers and wind protection
- Cost: $80-150 for traditional insulation materials

Heat Source Safety & Management
Fire Safety Equipment

- Fire extinguisher: ABC-rated extinguisher suitable for all fire types
- Fire blanket: A Smothering blanket for clothing fires and small blazes
- Smoke detectors: Battery-powered detectors for enclosed shelter areas
- Escape planning: Multiple exit routes planned and practiced with family
- Cost: $60-120 for a complete fire safety system

Fuel Storage & Management

- Propane storage: Outdoor storage only, secured from tampering
- Fuel rotation: Use the oldest fuel first, and replace expired or degraded supplies
- Leak detection: Soapy water solution for checking propane connections
- Safety distances: Maintain proper distances between fuel storage and ignition sources
- Cost: Safety equipment and storage containers $40-80

Emergency Heating Improvisation
Improvised Heat Sources (Emergency Only)

- Candle heaters: Multiple candles in metal containers with heat-safe surfaces
- Alcohol burners: Improvised burners using rubbing alcohol in metal containers

- Body heat conservation: Sharing warmth through close contact and shared insulation
- Exercise heating: Planned physical activity to generate internal body heat
- Cost: Improvised systems use available materials, with minimal additional cost

Heat Conservation Strategies

- Smaller spaces: Heat smaller areas rather than attempting to warm large spaces
- Heat capture: Use barriers and reflectors to direct heat toward occupied areas
- Activity planning: Schedule physical activity during the coldest periods
- Clothing systems: Layer management to optimize personal thermal regulation
- Cost: Primarily operational strategies rather than equipment purchases

Chapter Summary: Building Your Family's Shelter & Warmth Security

Comprehensive shelter and warmth systems provide the physical protection and thermal regulation that keep your family safe, comfortable, and functional regardless of housing situation or weather conditions. By implementing the systems in this chapter, you'll have:

✓ **Professional temporary shelter capability** with weather-rated tents and versatile tarp systems

✓ **Quality sleep systems** maintain rest and recovery during high-stress situations

✓ **Layered clothing systems** providing precise temperature control in any weather condition

✓ **Safe heating solutions** maintain comfortable temperatures without carbon monoxide risk

✓ **Insulation strategies** maximizing heat retention and minimizing fuel requirements

✓ **Emergency improvisation knowledge,** adapting available materials for shelter and warmth needs

Implementation Priority Order:

1. Basic shelter system (tent, ground protection, sleeping bags, pads)
2. Climate-appropriate clothing with proper layering systems
3. Safe heating equipment with fuel supply and safety equipment
4. Insulation materials and heat conservation systems
5. Comfort items and sleep enhancement accessories
6. Advanced shelter systems and backup/redundancy equipment

Budget-Friendly Implementation Strategy:

- **Phase 1** (Months 1-2): Basic tent and sleeping systems ($600-1,000)
- **Phase 2** (Months 3-4): Clothing layers and weather protection ($400-800)
- **Phase 3** (Months 5-6): Heating systems and insulation materials ($300-600)
- **Total Investment**: $1,300-2,400 for a complete family shelter and warmth capability

System Integration Benefits:

- Shelter systems work in home, evacuation, and camping scenarios
- Clothing layers adapt to indoor and outdoor temperature management
- Heating systems provide backup when the primary building heating fails
- Sleep systems maintain rest quality regardless of location or conditions

Climate Adaptation Considerations:

- Cold climates: Emphasize insulation, heating capacity, and wind

protection
- Hot climates: Focus on ventilation, shade systems, and cooling strategies
- Wet climates: Prioritize waterproofing and moisture management
- Variable climates: Build systems that adapt to seasonal temperature ranges

Safety Prioritization:

- Carbon monoxide prevention through proper ventilation and CO detectors
- Fire safety with extinguishers, detectors, and escape planning
- Hypothermia prevention through proper insulation and heat sources
- Structural safety with proper shelter setup and site selection

Shelter Versatility Planning:

- Home use: Backup heating and insulation for power outages
- Evacuation scenarios: Portable systems for temporary relocation
- Vehicle camping: Systems that work in cars, RVs, or temporary structures
- Outdoor scenarios: Weather protection for extended outdoor operations

Now that your physical safety and comfort are secured through shelter and warmth systems, we'll address hygiene and sanitation systems that maintain health and dignity when normal water and waste systems are unavailable.

Chapter 7

Chapter 7: Hygiene & Sanitation Systems

"Maintaining cleanliness and preventing illness are crucial when regular services are disrupted and medical care may not be readily available."

Hygiene and sanitation serve as the invisible foundation of health, becoming critically important when regular water, sewer, and waste management systems fail. Poor sanitation can cause disease outbreaks that are more dangerous than the original emergency. Professional hygiene systems help maintain health, dignity, and morale, while preventing secondary disasters that often follow infrastructure failures. This chapter outlines comprehensive sanitation systems that keep your family healthy and comfortable, no matter the service disruptions.

7.1 Personal Hygiene Systems

Personal cleanliness prevents illness, maintains psychological well-being, and fosters social cohesion during high-stress emergency situations. Strategic hygiene systems operate effectively with limited water while maintaining health standards.

Body Cleaning & Maintenance

Soap & Cleaning Systems Effective cleaning requires appropriate soaps that work in cold water and limited quantities while remaining gentle on skin during frequent use.

Biodegradable Soap Collection

- Bar soap: 8 bars biodegradable soap (4 oz bars, 2 per person per month)
- Liquid hand soap: 2 pump bottles (16 oz each) for frequent hand washing
- Body wash concentrate: 2 bottles of concentrated soap for efficient water use
- Dish soap: 2 bottles of biodegradable dish soap for utensil and cookware cleaning
- Cost: $25-40 for a complete family soap supply

Soap Selection Criteria

- Biodegradable formula: Safe for gray water disposal and environmental protection
- Multi-purpose capability: Body, hair, and dish cleaning to reduce inventory
- Cold water effectiveness: Works efficiently in unheated water
- Concentrated formulas: Maximum cleaning per ounce to reduce storage requirements
- Antimicrobial properties: Added protection against bacterial contamination

Hair Care & Grooming

Hair Maintenance Systems: Clean hair prevents scalp infections and maintains psychological well-being during extended emergency periods.

Shampoo & Conditioning

- Shampoo: 2 bottles (16 oz each) concentrated or 2-in-1 formula
- Dry shampoo: 2 cans for water-free hair cleaning when water is scarce
- Conditioner: 1 bottle of leave-in conditioner for damaged or dry hair

- Comb/brush set: 4 personal grooming tools for individual use
- Cost: $20-35 for a complete family hair care system

Water-Conservation Hair Care

- No-rinse shampoos: Foam cleansers that require no water for removal
- Hair ties and clips: Keep hair clean and out of the face during work activities
- Head coverings: Bandanas and hats extend the time between hair washing
- Scalp wipes: Pre-moistened wipes for quick scalp cleaning without water
- Cost: $15-25 for water-conservation hair care accessories

Oral Hygiene Maintenance

Dental Care Systems Oral health prevents serious infections that can become life-threatening when medical care is unavailable.

Complete Dental Care Kit

- Toothbrushes: 4 primary plus four backup toothbrushes (soft bristles preferred)
- Toothpaste: 4 tubes (6 oz each) of fluoride toothpaste for cavity prevention
- Dental floss: 4 packs of unwaxed floss plus two floss picks for convenience
- Mouthwash: 2 bottles of antiseptic mouthwash for bacterial control
- Cost: $25-40 for a complete family dental care system

Alternative Oral Care Methods

- Baking soda: Multi-purpose tooth cleaning and breath freshening
- A saltwater rinse: Natural antiseptic using stored salt and clean water
- Chew sticks: A Traditional tooth cleaning method using fibrous wood

- Xylitol gum: Sugar-free gum that promotes oral health and fresh breath
- Cost: $10-20 for alternative oral care materials

Body Odor & Perspiration Management

Deodorant & Antiperspirant Systems Body odor control maintains social relationships and prevents bacterial infections in skin folds.

Deodorant Collection

- Stick deodorants: 4 individual deodorants (one per person)
- Powder deodorants: 2 containers of talc-free powder for foot and body use
- Wet wipes: Body cleansing wipes for quick freshening between full cleaning
- Antibacterial hand gel: 2 bottles (8 oz each) alcohol-based sanitizer
- Cost: $20-35 for a complete odor control system

Towels & Drying Systems

Efficient Drying & Comfort Proper drying prevents bacterial growth and maintains skin health during limited washing opportunities.

Towel Systems

- Bath towels: 4 full-size absorbent towels (one per person)
- Quick-dry towels: 4 microfiber travel towels for rapid drying and compact storage
- Washcloths: 8 small cloths for targeted cleaning and face washing
- Paper towels: 6 rolls for disposable cleaning and drying applications
- Cost: $40-70 for a complete family drying system

Towel Maintenance

- Washing system: Portable washboard or collapsible basin for towel cleaning
- Clothesline: 50 feet of rope plus 50 clothespins for towel drying

- Disinfection: Bleach solution for sanitizing towels between uses
- Rotation schedule: Multiple towels allow proper drying between uses
- Cost: $20-35 for towel maintenance equipment

7.2 Waste Management Systems

Effective waste management prevents disease transmission, controls odors, and maintains sanitary living conditions when normal sewer and garbage systems become unavailable.

Human Waste Management

Toilet Systems for Non-Functioning Plumbing

Human waste poses the greatest health risk and requires immediate, effective management solutions.

Portable Toilet Systems

- Camping toilet: 1 portable camping toilet with 5-gallon waste capacity
- Toilet seat adapter: Fits on a 5-gallon bucket for emergency toilet conversion
- Privacy shelter: Pop-up shelter or heavy-duty tarp for bathroom privacy
- Toilet paper: 16 rolls biodegradable toilet paper (1 roll per person per week)
- Cost: $60-120 for a complete portable toilet system

Waste Container & Bag System

- Waste bags: 100 biodegradable waste bags specifically designed for human waste
- Bucket system: 5-gallon buckets with tight-fitting lids for waste collection
- Absorbent material: 10 lbs of cat litter or sawdust for odor control and absorption
- Disinfectant: 2 bottles of toilet bowl cleaner for container sanitization
- Cost: $40-80 for waste collection and odor control materials

Waste Treatment & Disposal

Safe Waste Processing Proper waste treatment prevents groundwater contamination and disease transmission.

Composting Toilet Systems (Advanced)

- Composting unit: Self-contained composting toilet for permanent installation
- Carbon materials: Sawdust, peat moss, or shredded paper for the carbon balance
- Ventilation system: Fan and ductwork for odor control and proper decomposition
- Maintenance supplies: pH testing strips and compost thermometer
- Cost: $200-600 for a complete composting toilet system

Latrine Construction Materials

- Digging tools: Folding shovel and pickaxe for latrine excavation
- Lime: Hydrated lime for waste treatment and odor control
- Screening: Hardware cloth for fly and pest control over waste areas
- Marking supplies: Stakes and flagging tape for latrine area identification
- Cost: $40-80 for latrine construction and maintenance materials

Gray Water Management

Wastewater from Washing & Cleaning Gray water management prevents standing water that breeds mosquitoes and bacteria while potentially providing irrigation water.

Gray Water Collection Systems

- Collection basins: 3 collapsible basins for dishwater and wash water collection
- Filtration system: Simple screen filters to remove food particles and soap residue
- Storage containers: 5-gallon containers for gray water storage and

transport
- Distribution system: Watering cans or a gravity-feed system for plant irrigation
- Cost: $30-60 for gray water collection and reuse system

Gray Water Treatment

- Biodegradable soaps: Ensure all cleaning products are safe for soil disposal
- Grease separation: Simple grease traps prevent soil contamination from cooking oils
- pH adjustment: Lime or vinegar to adjust gray water pH for plant compatibility
- Mulch basins: Wood chips or straw for gray water filtration before soil absorption
- Cost: $20-40 for gray water treatment materials

Garbage & Solid Waste Management

Trash Collection & Storage Solid waste management prevents pest attraction and disease transmission while maintaining sanitary living conditions.

Waste Storage Systems

- Heavy-duty trash bags: 100 bags (30 to 45-gallon capacity) for solid waste collection
- Trash containers: 2 containers with tight-fitting lids for odor and pest control
- Bag ties: 100 zip ties or twist ties for secure bag closure
- Compaction tools: Manual trash compactor or simple crushing methods
- Cost: $25-50 for solid waste collection and storage

Waste Reduction Strategies

- Composting system: Kitchen scrap composting for organic waste reduction
- Burning barrel: Safe burning container for combustible waste (where legal)
- Recycling separation: Sort materials for potential reuse or recycling when services resume
- Packaging reduction: Choose products with minimal packaging to reduce waste volume
- Cost: $30-70 for waste reduction equipment and systems

7.3 Cleaning & Disinfection Systems

Comprehensive cleaning and disinfection prevent disease transmission and maintain healthy living environments when normal cleaning services and supplies become unavailable.

Surface Cleaning & Disinfection
Multi-Surface Cleaning Systems. Effective surface cleaning removes contamination and prevents bacterial growth on commonly touched surfaces.

Disinfectant Solutions

- Hand sanitizer: 4 bottles (16 oz each) alcohol-based sanitizer ($\geq 60\%$ alcohol)
- Surface disinfectant: 2 cans of aerosol disinfectant for quick surface treatment
- Bleach solution: 1-gallon unscented bleach for mixing custom disinfectant solutions
- Disinfectant wipes: 400 pre-moistened wipes for convenient surface cleaning
- Cost: $30-50 for a complete disinfection supply system

Cleaning Solution Preparation

- Bleach ratios: 1 tablespoon bleach per gallon of water for general disinfection
- Alcohol solutions: 70% isopropyl alcohol for equipment and skin disinfection
- Soap solutions: Concentrated dish soap for general cleaning and degreasing
- Vinegar solutions: White vinegar for natural cleaning and mineral deposit removal
- Cost: Base chemicals cost $10-20, primarily knowledge-based preparation

Cleaning Tools & Equipment
Mechanical Cleaning Systems. Proper cleaning tools enable effective removal of contamination and maintenance of sanitary conditions.
Cleaning Tool Collection

- Microfiber cloths: 8 cloths for effective cleaning without scratching surfaces
- Scrub brushes: 4 brushes (various stiffness) for different cleaning applications
- Mop system: 1 mop with washable mop heads for floor cleaning
- Bucket system: 2 buckets for clean and dirty water separation during mopping
- Cost: $40-70 for a complete mechanical cleaning system

Specialized Cleaning Equipment

- Toilet brush: 2 brushes dedicated to toilet and bathroom cleaning
- Bottle brushes: 4 brushes for cleaning narrow containers and bottles
- Scouring pads: Non-scratch pads for cookware and delicate surface cleaning
- Rubber gloves: 8 pairs of chemical-resistant gloves for cleaning protection

- Cost: $20-35 for specialized cleaning tools

Air Quality & Ventilation

Indoor Air Management. Air quality control prevents respiratory problems and reduces disease transmission in enclosed living spaces.

Ventilation Systems

- Battery-powered fans: 2 fans for air circulation in enclosed spaces
- Air filters: HEPA filters for air purification systems, if available
- Exhaust fans: Portable ventilation for removing contaminated air
- Natural ventilation: Window and door management for airflow optimization
- Cost: $60-150 for mechanical air circulation equipment

Air Purification Methods

- Activated charcoal: Odor absorption and air filtering material
- Essential oils: Natural antimicrobial compounds for air freshening
- UV sanitizers: Portable UV lights for air and surface disinfection
- Salt lamps: Natural ionization for air quality improvement
- Cost: $40-100 for natural air purification materials

7.4 Laundry & Clothing Care

Clean clothing prevents skin infections, maintains insulation properties, and supports psychological well-being during extended emergency periods.

Water-Efficient Washing Systems

Manual Laundry Methods Manual washing systems clean clothing effectively while conserving water and working without electrical power.

Portable Washing Equipment

- Washboard: 1 traditional washboard for manual clothes washing
- Wash basin: 2 large collapsible basins for washing and rinsing water

- Plunger washer: Manual agitation device for more effective cleaning
- Wash bags: 4 mesh bags for washing delicate items and organizing laundry
- Cost: $40-80 for a complete manual washing system

Laundry Detergent Systems

- Powdered detergent: 2 lbs concentrated powder for cold water effectiveness
- Laundry bar soap: 4 bars of traditional laundry soap for heavy-duty cleaning
- Fabric softener: Vinegar solution for natural fabric softening
- Stain treatment: Hydrogen peroxide and baking soda for stain removal
- Cost: $15-30 for laundry cleaning supplies

Drying & Clothing Care

Clothing Drying Systems Proper drying prevents mildew, bacterial growth, and fabric damage while maintaining clothing functionality.

Clothesline Systems

- Clothesline rope: 100 feet of heavy-duty rope for outdoor clothes drying
- Clothespins: 100 wooden or plastic pins for secure clothing attachment
- Drying rack: 1 collapsible indoor drying rack for weather protection
- Pulley system: Rope and pulley system for high-line drying in a limited space
- Cost: $25-50 for a complete clothes drying system

Clothing Maintenance

- Sewing kit: Needles, thread, buttons, and patches for clothing repair
- Fabric scissors: Sharp scissors for cutting fabric and thread
- Iron alternatives: Heavy pot or smooth stone for pressing clothing

- Moth prevention: Cedar blocks or lavender sachets for clothing storage
- Cost: $20-40 for clothing maintenance and repair supplies

Fabric Care & Storage
Clean Clothing Storage Proper storage prevents contamination of clean clothes and extends clothing life between washings.
Storage Systems

- Plastic storage bins: 4 bins with tight lids for clean clothing protection
- Vacuum bags: Space-saving storage for seasonal or backup clothing
- Cedar sachets: Natural moth and insect repellent for clothing storage
- Moisture control: Silica gel packets or other desiccants prevent mildew
- Cost: $30-60 for clothing storage and protection systems

Clothing Inventory Management

- Rotation system: Clean, wearing, and dirty clothing cycle management
- Inventory lists: Track clothing items and their condition
- Repair priorities: Identify and prioritize clothing repairs needed
- Replacement planning: Identify clothing items that need replacement
- Cost: Primarily organizational time investment

Personal Clothing Hygiene
Underwear & Sock Management Undergarments require frequent changing and careful hygiene management to prevent infections and maintain comfort.
Undergarment Supplies

- Extra underwear: 14 pairs per person for daily changes during an emergency
- Extra socks: 20 pairs per person (various weights and materials)
- Bras/undershirts: 7 per person for weekly rotation schedule
- Sleepwear: 3 sets per person for comfort and hygiene separation

- Cost: $100-200 per person for an adequate undergarment supply

Feminine Hygiene Systems

- Sanitary pads: 4 packs (14 pads per pack) for a complete monthly supply
- Tampons: 2 boxes (20 count each) for alternative protection
- Panty liners: 2 packs for daily freshness and light protection
- Feminine wipes: 4 packs for convenient feminine cleaning
- Cost: $25-50 for a complete feminine hygiene supply

Chapter Summary: Building Your Family's Hygiene & Sanitation Independence

Comprehensive hygiene and sanitation systems maintain health, prevent disease transmission, and preserve dignity when normal water and waste services become unavailable. By implementing the systems in this chapter, you'll have:

✓ **Complete personal hygiene capability** with water-efficient cleaning systems and supplies

✓ **Professional waste management** prevents disease transmission and environmental contamination

✓ **Effective cleaning and disinfection,** maintaining sanitary living conditions

✓ **Sustainable laundry systems** keep clothing clean and functional

✓ **Odor and pest control,** maintaining comfortable and healthy living environments

✓ **Privacy and dignity preservation** through proper facilities and procedures

Implementation Priority Order:

1. Personal hygiene supplies (soap, toothpaste, deodorant, towels)
2. Human waste management systems (portable toilet, waste bags, absorbent materials)
3. Cleaning and disinfection supplies (sanitizers, disinfectants, cleaning

tools)
4. Laundry systems (manual washing equipment, drying systems, detergent)
5. Advanced waste treatment (composting systems, gray water management)
6. Air quality and ventilation systems

Budget-Friendly Implementation Strategy:

- **Phase 1** (Month 1): Personal hygiene basics and waste management ($150-250)
- **Phase 2** (Month 2): Cleaning supplies and laundry systems ($100-200)
- **Phase 3** (Month 3): Advanced systems and backup supplies ($100-200)
- **Total Investment**: $350-650 for complete family hygiene and sanitation capability

Health & Safety Priorities:

- **Disease prevention**: Proper hand washing and surface disinfection protocols
- **Waste isolation**: Safe handling and disposal of human waste materials
- **Water quality**: Preventing contamination of drinking water supplies
- **Pest control**: Eliminating breeding grounds for disease-carrying insects
- **Air quality**: Maintaining breathable air in enclosed living spaces

System Integration Benefits:

- Graywater reuse reduces freshwater consumption for irrigation
- Composting systems turn waste into valuable soil amendment
- Cleaning supply consolidation reduces storage requirements
- Manual systems work without electricity or running water

Privacy & Dignity Considerations:

- Portable privacy shelters for bathroom facilities
- Personal hygiene supplies for individual family members
- Clothing care systems maintain a normal appearance
- Odor control prevents social embarrassment and health issues

Water Conservation Strategies:

- Efficient washing techniques minimize water usage
- Gray water collection and reuse systems
- Waterless cleaning alternatives (wipes, dry shampoo, sanitizers)
- Priority water allocation for critical hygiene needs

Waste Stream Management:

- Separation of different waste types for appropriate treatment
- Volume reduction through composting and waste minimization
- Safe storage prevents pest attraction and disease transmission
- Long-term disposal planning for extended emergencies

With health and hygiene secured, we'll address the documentation and financial systems that enable recovery, insurance claims, and legal continuity when normal record-keeping and banking services become disrupted.

Chapter 8

Important Documents & Financial Resources

"Preserving vital records and having accessible cash ensures you can prove identity, access resources, and transact when electronic systems are down."

When disasters happen, the ability to confirm identity, access financial resources, and show ownership often influences recovery speed and insurance claims. Digital systems fail, banks shut down, and paper records get lost—but families with thorough document protection and alternative financial options stay legally connected and resourceful during any crisis. This chapter develops document preservation and financial systems that work when regular systems fail.

8.1 Critical Document Protection

Document security goes beyond simple storage to create multiple backup systems that preserve legal identity, ownership proof, and essential information regardless of destruction or system failures.

Identity & Legal Documents

Core Identity Documentation Identity documents enable access to services, prove legal status, and establish eligibility for assistance during recovery operations.

Essential Identity Papers (Originals & Certified Copies)

- Driver's licenses/state IDs: 4 current licenses plus photocopies
- Passports: Up to 4 current passports plus certified copy pages
- Birth certificates: 4 certified copies (not hospital certificates)
- Social Security cards: 4 original cards plus laminated photocopies
- Marriage certificate: 1 original plus three certified copies
- Cost: $200-400 for a complete certified document collection

Document Authentication Requirements

- Certified copies: Official government-issued copies with raised seals
- Notarized copies: Notary-verified copies for legal acceptance
- Apostille certification: International document authentication if needed
- Translation services: Certified translation of foreign-language documents
- Document verification: Contact issuing agencies to verify authenticity requirements

Property & Asset Documentation

Ownership & Insurance Proof Property documentation establishes ownership, enables insurance claims, and proves asset value for recovery assistance.

Real Estate Documentation

- Property deeds: 1 original deed plus 2 certified copies
- Mortgage documents: Current mortgage statements and payment records
- Property tax records: 3 years of tax assessments and payment receipts
- Homeowner's insurance: Declaration pages and full policy documentation
- Cost: Document copies $50-100, primarily organizational effort

Vehicle Documentation

- Vehicle titles: Originals for each family vehicle
- Vehicle registration: Current registration plus renewal documentation
- Auto insurance: Declaration pages and full policy coverage details
- Loan documentation: Auto loan papers and payment records
- Cost: $20-50 for certified copies and documentation organization

Personal Property Documentation

- Home inventory: Detailed list with photographs of valuable items
- Serial numbers: Electronics, appliances, tools, and valuable equipment
- Purchase receipts: Major purchases, warranties, and service records
- Appraisal documents: Professional valuations of jewelry, art, collectibles
- Cost: $50-150 for professional appraisal services if needed

Financial & Legal Records

Financial Account Documentation Financial records enable account access, establish ownership, and provide transaction history for recovery planning.

Banking & Investment Records

- Bank statements: 6 months current statements for all accounts
- Investment accounts: Brokerage statements, retirement account summaries
- Credit card information: Account numbers, customer service contacts
- Loan documents: Personal loans, student loans, mortgage papers
- Cost: Primarily organizational effort, with some account research fees possible

Legal & Estate Documentation

- Wills & trusts: Original documents plus copies stored separately
- Power of attorney: Financial and healthcare POA documents
- Healthcare directives: Living wills, DNR orders, medical power of attorney
- Guardianship papers: Legal guardianship documents for minor children
- Cost: $500-1,500 for professional legal document preparation

Medical & Health Records

Health Information Systems Medical records enable continued healthcare, medication access, and treatment continuity when normal medical systems are disrupted.

Medical Record Documentation

- Medical history summaries: 4 copies of a comprehensive health history
- Prescription lists: Current medications with dosages and prescribing doctors
- Vaccination records: Complete immunization history for all family members
- Allergy information: Detailed allergy lists and reaction severity
- Cost: $50-100 for medical record copying and organization

Healthcare Provider Information

- Doctor contact lists: Primary care physicians, specialists, pharmacies
- Hospital preferences: Preferred hospitals and emergency contact procedures
- Insurance information: Healthcare insurance cards and policy details
- Medical power of attorney: Healthcare decision-making authorization
- Cost: Organizational time investment

8.2 Digital Backup Strategies

Digital document storage creates instantly accessible backups that survive physical document destruction while providing searchable, shareable copies for remote access.

Encrypted Storage Systems
Secure Digital Document Storage
Digital backups must balance accessibility with security to prevent identity theft while ensuring emergency access.
Encrypted USB Drive Systems

- Encrypted drives: 2 USB drives (64GB each) with hardware encryption
- Document scanning: High-resolution PDF scans of all critical documents
- Encryption software: Military-grade encryption for sensitive document protection
- Access codes: Secure password system enabling family member access
- Cost: $80-150 for encrypted USB drives and scanning equipment

Cloud Storage Integration

- Secure cloud service: Encrypted cloud storage with two-factor authentication
- Document synchronization: Automatic backup of scanned documents
- Access management: Family member access controls and sharing permissions
- Offline access: Downloaded copies available without an internet connection
- Cost: $50-100 annually for secure cloud storage services

Document Digitization Process
High-Quality Document Scanning Professional document scanning creates legally acceptable digital copies while preserving original document

integrity.

Scanning Equipment & Process

- Document scanner: High-resolution scanner capable of legal-quality copies
- Scanning software: PDF creation with optical character recognition (OCR)
- File organization: Systematic naming and folder structure for quick retrieval
- Quality control: Verification that scanned copies are complete and legible
- Cost: $150-300 for a professional-grade document scanner

Digital File Management

- Naming conventions: Consistent file names enabling quick identification
- Folder structure: Logical organization by document type and family member
- Backup verification: Regular checking that files remain accessible and uncorrupted
- Update procedures: Systematic replacement of outdated documents
- Cost: Primarily organizational time investment

Smartphone & Mobile Access

Mobile Document Storage Smartphone storage provides immediate document access during emergencies when computers and the internet may not be available.

Mobile Documentation Apps

- Secure document apps: Password-protected apps for sensitive document storage
- Photo storage: High-resolution photographs of critical documents

- Offline access: Documents available without a cellular or internet connection
- Quick retrieval: Search and organization features for rapid document location
- Cost: $20-50 annually for premium document management apps

Emergency Information Cards

- Wallet cards: Laminated cards with essential contact and medical information
- Emergency contacts: Key phone numbers and addresses in compact format
- Medical alerts: Critical medical information for first responders
- Account information: Abbreviated financial account information for emergency access
- Cost: $10-20 for lamination and printing

8.3 Cash & Alternative Financial Instruments

Physical currency and alternative financial tools provide transaction capability when electronic payment systems fail, and banks become inaccessible.

Strategic Cash Management

Emergency Cash Reserves

Cash offers instant buying power and transaction ability when electronic systems fail during widespread emergencies.

Cash Denomination Strategy

- Small bills priority: $400-500 in $1, $5, and $10 denominations
- Medium bills: $200-300 in $20 bills for larger purchases
- Large bills: $100-200 in $50 and $100 bills for major expenses
- Coin collection: $50-100 in quarters, dimes, and nickels for exact change
- Cost: $750-1,100 total emergency cash reserve

Cash Storage & Security

- Multiple locations: Divide cash among home, vehicle, and workplace locations
- Waterproof storage: Vacuum-sealed bags protecting cash from moisture damage
- Fireproof storage: Fire-resistant document safe for primary cash storage
- Concealed storage: Hidden storage locations prevent theft discovery
- Cost: $100-250 for secure cash storage systems

Alternative Payment Methods
Non-Bank Financial Instruments

Alternative payment methods provide financial access when traditional banking systems become unavailable.

Prepaid Financial Cards

- Prepaid debit cards: $200-500 balance on major network cards (Visa/MasterCard)
- Gift cards: $200-300 on major retailer cards (grocery stores, gas stations, pharmacies)
- Reloadable cards: Cards that can be reloaded when banking systems resume
- Card documentation: Account numbers and customer service contacts for card management
- Cost: Face value of cards plus minimal activation fees

Precious Metals (Advanced Strategy)

- Silver coins: 20-50 one-ounce silver coins for medium-value transactions
- Gold coins: 2-5 one-ounce gold coins for high-value transactions or wealth preservation

- Fractional metals: Smaller denomination precious metals for precise transactions
- Authentication: Precious metal testing kit to verify authenticity
- Cost: Market value plus premium for coins (typically 5-10% over spot price)

Banking Relationship Management

Multi-Bank Strategy Multiple banking relationships prevent single-point financial failure when specific banks become unavailable.

Primary Banking Relationships

- Primary bank: Main checking and savings accounts with local branch access
- Secondary bank: Backup accounts at different institution for redundancy
- Credit union membership: An Alternative financial institution with a different operating model
- Online banking: An Internet-only bank for additional account diversification
- Cost: Minimal account maintenance fees, typically under $50 monthly total

Emergency Banking Access

- Account documentation: Account numbers, routing numbers, online access credentials
- Customer service contacts: 24-hour banking customer service phone numbers
- Branch locations: Multiple branch locations and ATM networks identified
- Wire transfer capability: International wire transfer procedures and codes
- Cost: Research and documentation time investment

Financial Communication Systems

Emergency Financial Contacts Reliable financial communication enables resource access and account management during disrupted communications.

Financial Institution Contacts

- Bank contact lists: Customer service, branch managers, loan officers
- Investment advisors: Financial planners, investment account managers, retirement account administrators
- Insurance agents: Property, auto, life, and health insurance representatives
- Legal advisors: Estate attorneys, tax preparers, financial legal counsel
- Cost: Contact list maintenance and periodic communication verification

Account Recovery Procedures

- Identity verification: Documentation required to re-establish account access
- Emergency procedures: Bank-specific procedures for emergency account access
- Beneficiary information: Account beneficiary contacts and procedures
- Power of attorney: Financial POA procedures for account management by others
- Cost: Legal consultation for POA preparation $200-500

8.4 Document Recovery & Legal Continuity

Legal continuity systems maintain family legal status, enable recovery assistance, and preserve rights when original documents are destroyed or officials are unavailable.

Document Replacement Procedures

Systematic Document Reconstruction: Document replacement procedures restore legal identity and property rights when original documents are destroyed.

Government Document Replacement

- Birth certificates: Contact the state vital records office with identification requirements
- Social Security cards: Social Security Administration replacement procedures
- Driver's licenses: State DMV replacement requirements and documentation
- Passport replacement: State Department emergency passport procedures
- Cost: $20-100 per document for expedited replacement services

Financial Document Reconstruction

- Bank account verification: Account reconstruction using available documentation
- Credit report access: Credit bureau reports establish financial history
- Insurance policy replacement: Insurance company policy reconstruction procedures
- Investment account recovery: Brokerage account recovery using a social security number and identification
- Cost: Credit reports $50-100, primarily administrative time investment

Legal Continuity Planning

Continuity of Legal Authority Legal authority systems ensure family decision-making continues when primary decision-makers become unavailable.

Power of Attorney Systems

- Financial power of attorney: Legal authority for financial decisions and account access

- Healthcare power of attorney: Medical decision-making authority for incapacitated family members
- Limited power of attorney: Specific authorization for defined situations and time periods
- Durable power of attorney: Authority that continues during incapacitation periods
- Cost: $300-800 for comprehensive power of attorney legal preparation

Guardianship & Family Continuity

- Minor child guardianship: Legal guardianship designation for minor children
- Temporary guardianship: Short-term care authorization during parent absence
- Pet care authorization: Legal authority for pet care and veterinary decisions
- Property management: Authority for property maintenance and management decisions
- Cost: $500-1,500 for comprehensive family legal continuity planning

Insurance & Recovery Documentation

Insurance Claim Preparation Pre-disaster documentation enables rapid insurance claims and maximum recovery payments.

Property Documentation for Claims

- Photo inventory: Room-by-room photographs of all property and possessions
- Video inventory: Walkthrough video documentation with narration describing items
- Receipt collection: Purchase receipts for major items and recent acquisitions
- Appraisal documentation: Professional appraisals for high-value items
- Cost: $100-500 for professional appraisals, primarily time investment

for photography

Insurance Policy Management

- Policy reviews: Annual review of coverage limits and policy terms
- Coverage verification: Confirmation that coverage matches current property values
- Claims procedures: Understanding of claims filing procedures and requirements
- Agent relationships: Regular communication with insurance agents and adjusters
- Cost: Policy premiums plus annual review consultations

Recovery Assistance Documentation

Disaster Recovery Eligibility Proper documentation establishes eligibility for government assistance, insurance payments, and disaster relief programs.

Government Assistance Documentation

- Income verification: Tax returns and income statements for assistance eligibility
- Property ownership proof: Documentation establishing property ownership and damage
- Loss documentation: Detailed records of disaster-related losses and damages
- Temporary assistance needs: Documentation of immediate housing, food, and medical needs
- Cost: Tax preparation and documentation organization time investment

Recovery Planning Documentation

- Contractor estimates: Professional damage assessments and repair

estimates
- Building permits: Documentation for reconstruction and repair authorizations
- Recovery timeline: Systematic planning for property restoration and family recovery
- Budget planning: Financial planning for recovery costs and timeline
- Cost: Professional assessments $200-1,000, planning consultation fees

Chapter Summary: Building Your Family's Document & Financial Security

Comprehensive document protection and financial preparedness provide the legal foundation and resource access that enable rapid recovery and maintain family stability during and after emergencies. By implementing the systems in this chapter, you'll have:

✓ **Complete identity documentation** with originals and certified copies protected from destruction

✓ **Digital backup systems** providing instant access to critical documents from any location

✓ **Strategic cash reserves** enabling transactions when electronic payment systems fail

✓ **Alternative financial instruments** providing payment options beyond traditional banking

✓ **Legal continuity systems** maintaining family authority and decision-making capability

✓ **Recovery documentation** enabling rapid insurance claims and assistance program access

Implementation Priority Order:

1. Gather and organize critical identity and property documents
2. Create secure digital backups with encryption and cloud storage
3. Establish emergency cash reserves in appropriate denominations
4. Set up alternative financial instruments (prepaid cards, secondary bank accounts)

5. Prepare legal continuity documents (power of attorney, wills, healthcare directives)
6. Create comprehensive insurance documentation and recovery planning

Budget-Friendly Implementation Strategy:

- **Phase 1** (Month 1): Document collection and basic digital backups ($200-400)
- **Phase 2** (Month 2): Emergency cash reserves and storage systems ($800-1,200)
- **Phase 3** (Month 3): Legal continuity documents and professional consultations ($500-1,000)
- **Total Investment**: $1,500-2,600 for complete document and financial security

Document Security Priorities:

- **Physical protection**: Fire-resistant, waterproof storage for original documents
- **Digital redundancy**: Multiple backup systems prevent data loss
- **Access control**: Security measures preventing unauthorized access while enabling family use
- **Regular updates**: Systematic replacement of outdated documents and information

Financial Access Strategies:

- **Multi-layered approach**: Cash, cards, banking, and alternative instruments
- **Geographic distribution**: Financial resources accessible from multiple locations
- **Institution diversification**: Multiple banks and financial relation-

ships
- **Recovery planning**: Systems enabling rapid financial recovery after disasters

Legal Continuity Benefits:

- **Decision-making authority**: Legal authorization for family members to act during emergencies
- **Healthcare continuity**: Medical decision-making capability when primary decision-makers are unavailable
- **Financial management**: Authority to access accounts and manage family finances
- **Property protection**: Legal authority to secure and maintain family property

Insurance Optimization:

- **Coverage verification**: Regular review ensuring adequate protection levels
- **Claims preparation**: Documentation enabling rapid and complete claims processing
- **Recovery planning**: Understanding of recovery procedures and assistance programs
- **Agent relationships**: Professional support for complex claims and recovery situations

Technology Integration:

- **Mobile access**: Critical documents available on smartphones for immediate access
- **Cloud synchronization**: Automatic backup ensuring the latest document versions
- **Encryption security**: Protection against identity theft and unautho-

CHAPTER 8

rized access
- **Offline capability**: Document access when internet and cellular services are unavailable

With legal and financial continuity secured, we'll address the specialized needs of different family members, including infants, seniors, pets, and family members with medical conditions or dietary requirements.

Chapter 9

Special Populations & Pets

"Tailoring your emergency supplies to individual needs ensures every family member—no matter their age, health status, or species—remains safe and comfortable during emergencies."

Emergency preparedness must consider the unique needs and vulnerabilities of each family member. Infants require specialized nutrition and care, seniors might need mobility assistance and complex medications, pets depend entirely on humans for their care, and family members with chronic conditions face serious risks if normal support systems break down. This chapter creates tailored preparedness plans to protect your family's most vulnerable members while preserving their dignity, comfort, and health during any emergency.

9.1 Infant & Child Specific Needs

Children face unique physiological and psychological vulnerabilities during emergencies. Their smaller body size, developing immune systems, and dependence on adults require specialized equipment, modified procedures, and child-focused comfort measures.

CHAPTER 9

Infant Nutrition & Feeding Systems

Complete Infant Feeding Independence Infant nutrition cannot be compromised or delayed—emergency feeding systems must provide complete nutritional independence regardless of availability of fresh foods or clean water.

Formula Feeding Systems

- Infant formula: 28-42 containers powdered formula (2-3 per day × 14 days)
- Ready-to-feed formula: 14 bottles liquid formula for water-shortage emergencies
- Feeding bottles: 10 bottles with different flow nipples for age-appropriate feeding
- Bottle cleaning supplies: Sterilizing tablets, bottle brushes, drying rack
- Cost: $200-350 for complete 14-day infant feeding system

Formula Preparation & Safety

- Water purification: Extra water purification capacity for formula preparation
- Measuring equipment: Precise measuring cups and spoons for proper mixing ratios
- Temperature testing: Thermometer strips for safe formula temperature verification
- Storage containers: Airtight storage for opened formula powder and prepared bottles
- Cost: $30-60 for formula preparation and safety equipment

Breastfeeding Support Systems

- Breast pump: Manual and electric breast pump options with battery backup

- Milk storage: Breast milk storage bags and labeling system for dated storage
- Nursing supplies: Lanolin, breast pads, nursing bras for extended breastfeeding periods
- Nutritional support: Extra calories and hydration for nursing mothers during stress
- Cost: $150-300 for comprehensive breastfeeding support system

Child Safety & Comfort Systems

Age-Appropriate Safety Equipment Children require specialized safety equipment that accounts for their size, developmental stage, and inability to manage complex safety procedures independently.

Infant Safety & Care

- Car seats: Emergency car seat plus installation equipment for evacuation vehicles
- Baby carriers: Multiple carrying systems for hands-free infant transport
- Diapers: 56 diapers (4 per day × 14 days) plus 25% buffer for illness
- Baby wipes: 4,000 wipes (200-300 per day during emergencies)
- Cost: $200-400 for a complete infant safety and care system

Toddler & School-Age Safety

- Child restraints: Age-appropriate car seats and booster seats for all vehicles
- ID systems: Laminated ID cards with photos, medical information, and emergency contacts
- Whistle necklaces: High-decibel whistles for signaling if separated from adults
- Comfort items: Familiar stuffed animals, blankets, or toys for psychological comfort
- Cost: $150-300 for child safety and identification systems

CHAPTER 9

Pediatric Medical & Health Needs

Child-Specific Medical Preparedness Children's medical needs differ significantly from adults in medication dosing, equipment sizing, and treatment approaches.

Pediatric Medication Systems

- Children's ibuprofen: 2 bottles (100mL each) for pain and fever management
- Acetaminophen suppositories: 20-count for children who cannot keep oral medication down
- Oral rehydration salts: Pediatric formulation for treating dehydration from illness
- Thermometer covers: 20 disposable covers for sanitary temperature monitoring
- Cost: $40-80 for pediatric medication emergency supply

Child Medical Equipment

- Pediatric masks: Child-sized N95 or surgical masks for respiratory protection
- Small blood pressure cuff: Child sized cuff for monitoring during illness
- Pulse oximeter: Pediatric sensors for oxygen level monitoring
- Nebulizer supplies: Child-sized masks and tubing for respiratory treatments
- Cost: $60-150 for pediatric medical monitoring equipment

Educational & Psychological Support

Learning Continuity & Mental Health Extended emergencies disrupt children's education and psychological stability—structured activities and familiar routines provide essential mental health support.

Educational Materials

- Workbooks: Age-appropriate educational workbooks for each child
- Art supplies: Crayons, colored pencils, paper, and drawing materials
- Reading materials: Familiar books plus new books for entertainment and education
- Educational games: Board games, puzzles, and learning activities
- Cost: $50-150 per child for educational and activity materials

Comfort & Routine Items

- Sleep comfort: Familiar pillows, blankets, and stuffed animals
- Routine items: Normal bedtime items, favorite cups, comfort objects
- Entertainment: Tablets with downloaded educational content and games (if power available)
- Music/audio: Battery-powered music player with familiar songs and audiobooks
- Cost: $100-250 per child for comfort and entertainment systems

9.2 Senior & Mobility Considerations

Older adults face unique challenges during emergencies, including mobility limitations, complex medication regimens, sensory impairments, and chronic health conditions that require specialized support and equipment.

Enhanced Medication Management

Complex Prescription Systems Seniors typically manage multiple medications with precise timing requirements—emergency systems must maintain medication schedules and provide backup access.

Advanced Medication Organization

- Weekly pill organizers: 4 large-compartment organizers allowing visual

verification of medication compliance
- Pill crusher: Manual pill crusher for seniors with swallowing difficulties
- Medication magnifier: Large-print labels and magnifying glass for accurate medication identification
- Backup prescriptions: 14-day supply plus contact information for prescribing physicians
- Cost: $60-120 for advanced medication management systems

Medication Safety & Monitoring

- Blood pressure monitoring: Automatic cuff with large display for self-monitoring
- Glucose monitoring: Extra test strips and backup glucose meter for diabetic seniors
- Medication interaction charts: Reference cards showing dangerous drug combinations
- Emergency medication information: Laminated cards with medication names, doses, and medical conditions
- Cost: $80-200 for medication monitoring and safety equipment

Mobility & Accessibility Support

Mobility Aid Systems Mobility equipment becomes critical during evacuations and extended emergencies when normal assistance may be unavailable.

Walking & Mobility Assistance

- Backup mobility aids: Extra cane tips, walker glides, crutch padding, wheelchair repair kit
- Mobility equipment batteries: Extra batteries for electric wheelchairs and scooters
- Transfer equipment: Sliding boards, transfer belts, and lifting aids for bed/chair transfers
- Grab bars: Portable grab bars that install without permanent mounting

- Cost: $100-300 for mobility aid backup and enhancement systems

Emergency Mobility Solutions

- Evacuation chair: A Lightweight chair for carrying mobility-impaired persons during evacuation
- Stair evacuation: Evacuation sleds or evacuation chairs for multi-story buildings
- Vehicle modifications: Temporary ramps, seat cushions, and transfer assistance equipment
- Communication aids: Whistle, bell, or electronic device for summoning assistance
- Cost: $200-600 for emergency mobility and evacuation equipment

Sensory & Communication Support

Vision & Hearing Assistance Sensory impairments create safety risks and communication challenges that require specialized equipment and procedures.

Vision Support Systems

- Extra eyeglasses: Backup prescription eyeglasses with current prescriptions
- Magnification aids: Handheld magnifiers and magnifying glasses for reading
- Lighting aids: High-intensity reading lights and task lighting for detailed work
- Large-print materials: Emergency procedures and contact information in large, clear print
- Cost: $150-350 for vision support and backup systems

Hearing Support Systems

- Hearing aid batteries: 30-day supply of batteries with battery tester
- Amplification devices: Personal amplifiers and assisted listening devices
- Visual alerts: Flashing light alerts for smoke detectors and emergency signals
- Communication boards: Picture boards and written communication aids for severe hearing loss
- Cost: $100-250 for hearing support and communication systems

Senior Health Monitoring

Health Status Assessment: Seniors' health can deteriorate rapidly during high-stress emergencies—monitoring systems provide early warning of medical problems.

Vital Sign Monitoring

- Blood pressure cuff: Large-display automatic cuff with memory function
- Pulse oximeter: Oxygen saturation monitoring for respiratory conditions
- Thermometer: Large-display digital thermometer with audio alerts
- Weight scale: Portable scale for monitoring fluid retention and medication effects
- Cost: $150-300 for comprehensive health monitoring equipment

Emergency Medical Communication

- Medical alert systems: Portable medical alert devices with GPS location capability
- Medical information cards: Waterproof cards with complete medical history and medication lists
- Healthcare provider contacts: 24-hour contact numbers for doctors, specialists, and pharmacies
- Insurance information: Medicare cards, supplemental insurance, and

prescription coverage information
- Cost: $50-150 for medical communication and identification systems

9.3 Pet Preparedness Planning

Pets depend entirely on human provision and cannot prepare for their own needs—comprehensive pet preparedness protects beloved family members while preventing pet-related delays during evacuations.

Pet Nutrition & Feeding Systems

Complete Pet Food Independence

Pet nutrition requirements are specific and cannot be easily substituted—emergency feeding systems must provide species-appropriate nutrition for extended periods.

Dog Feeding Systems (Medium Dog, 50 lbs.)

- Dry dog food: 35 lbs. high-quality dry food (2.5 lbs. per day × 14 days)
- Wet dog food: 28 cans (2 cans per day × 14 days) for variety and hydration
- Food storage: Airtight containers protect food from moisture and pests
- Feeding equipment: Collapsible bowls, measuring cups, food scoops
- Cost: $80-150 for a 14-day dog feeding system

Cat Feeding Systems (Indoor Cat, 10 lbs.)

- Dry cat food: 7 lbs. high-quality dry food (0.5 lbs. per day × 14 days)
- Wet cat food: 28 small cans (2 small cans per day × 14 days)
- Cat treats: Familiar treats for stress reduction and medication administration
- Water fountain: Battery-powered water fountain encouraging adequate hydration
- Cost: $60-120 for a 14-day cat feeding system

CHAPTER 9

Pet Health & Medical Care

Veterinary Medicine & First Aid Pet medical emergencies cannot wait for veterinary care—basic medical supplies and knowledge enable immediate treatment of injuries and common conditions.

Pet First Aid Supplies

- Bandages: Self-adhering bandages, gauze pads, and medical tape for wound care
- Antiseptics: Hydrogen peroxide, antibiotic ointment, and wound cleaning solutions
- Medications: Pain relievers, anti-diarrheal medication, and flea/tick prevention
- Thermometer: Digital pet thermometer with protective covers for health monitoring
- Cost: $50-100 for a comprehensive pet first aid kit

Prescription Pet Medications

- Regular medications: 14-day supply of all prescription medications plus dosing instructions
- Emergency medications: Anti-anxiety medication for stress-related behavioral problems
- Preventive medications: Heartworm prevention, flea/tick control, and vaccination records
- Medication administration: Pill guns, liquid medications, and treats for medication delivery
- Cost: $40-150, depending on specific pet medical needs

Pet Safety & Restraint Systems

Pet Transportation & Containment Pet safety during evacuations and temporary housing requires appropriate restraint systems that provide security while maintaining comfort.

Dog Restraint & Safety

- Harnesses: Well-fitting harnesses providing control without choking risk
- Leashes: 6-foot standard leash plus 20-foot-long line for temporary containment
- Collars: Backup collar with ID tags, including emergency contact information
- Crate/carrier: Appropriately sized transport crate for vehicle travel and temporary housing
- Cost: $80-200 for a complete dog restraint and transport system

Cat Restraint & Safety

- Cat carriers: Hard-sided carrier plus soft-sided backup for different transport needs
- Cat harness: Escape-proof harness for cats that might need supervised outdoor access
- ID collar: Breakaway collar with ID tags and microchip information
- Portable litter box: Collapsible litter box with 14-day supply of litter
- Cost: $60-150 for a complete cat restraint and containment system

Pet Comfort & Behavioral Management

Stress Reduction & Familiar Items. Pets experience severe stress during emergencies and disrupted routines—familiar items and comfort measures prevent behavioral problems and health issues.

Pet Comfort Systems

- Familiar bedding: Regular blankets, beds, or crate padding from the home environment
- Favorite toys: Familiar toys provide comfort and mental stimulation during stress
- Calming aids: Natural calming supplements or synthetic pheromone products
- Exercise equipment: Balls, rope toys, and interactive toys for mental and physical stimulation
- Cost: $40-100 for pet comfort and stress reduction systems

Waste Management & Hygiene

- Dog waste bags: 200 bags for waste pickup and disposal (14+ bags per day)
- Cat litter: 20 lbs. clumping litter plus scoop and disposal system
- Pet wipes: Cleaning wipes for pet hygiene when bathing is not possible
- Odor control: Enzymatic cleaners for accident cleanup and odor elimination
- Cost: $50-100 for pet waste management and hygiene supplies

9.4 Medical & Dietary Requirements

Family members with chronic medical conditions, dietary restrictions, or special needs require customized preparedness systems that maintain health and prevent medical emergencies when normal support systems fail.

Chronic Disease Management

Diabetes Management Systems Diabetes management becomes life-critical during emergencies when normal meal schedules, stress levels, and medical access change dramatically.

Advanced Diabetes Supplies

- Blood glucose monitoring: Extra glucose meter, test strips for 200+ tests, backup batteries
- Glucose management: Glucose tablets, glucagon emergency kit, complex carbohydrate sources
- Insulin storage: Insulin cooling case, extra insulin pens, needle disposal system
- Ketone monitoring: Ketone test strips for monitoring diabetic ketoacidosis risk
- Cost: $200-400 for comprehensive diabetes emergency management

Cardiovascular Disease Support

- Blood pressure monitoring: Automatic cuff with memory function and large display
- Medication management: Precise pill organizers with backup medications
- Activity monitoring: Pulse oximeter and heart rate monitor for activity guidelines
- Emergency medications: Nitroglycerin, aspirin, and emergency cardiac medication protocols
- Cost: $150-350 for cardiovascular emergency monitoring and support

Respiratory Condition Management

Asthma & COPD Support Systems Respiratory conditions can become life-threatening rapidly during emergencies, especially with poor air quality from fires, dust, or other environmental factors.

Advanced Respiratory Support

- Inhaler systems: Primary inhalers plus backup inhalers with spacer devices
- Nebulizer equipment: Battery-powered nebulizer with medication supplies and backup batteries

- Peak flow monitoring: Peak flow meter for objective breathing assessment
- Air quality protection: N95 masks, air purifiers, and indoor air quality management
- Cost: $200-500 for comprehensive respiratory emergency support

Oxygen Support Systems

- Portable oxygen: Battery-powered oxygen concentrator with backup batteries
- Oxygen supplies: Extra nasal cannulas, tubing, and oxygen delivery equipment
- Pulse oximetry: Continuous oxygen level monitoring with alarms
- Backup power: Extended battery systems for oxygen equipment during power outages
- Cost: $400-1,200 for oxygen support backup systems

Dietary Restriction Management

Specialized Diet Requirements

Medical diets cannot be compromised during emergencies—specialized food systems maintain health while providing adequate nutrition during stressful periods.

Gluten-Free Diet Systems

- Certified foods: 14-day supply of certified gluten-free grains, proteins, and processed foods
- Cooking separation: Dedicated cookware and utensils prevent cross-contamination
- Label reading: Magnifying glass and reference cards for identifying hidden gluten sources
- Symptom management: Medications for accidental gluten exposure and digestive support

- Cost: $200-400 for gluten-free emergency food supply (typically 30-50% premium over standard foods)

Renal Diet Management

- Low-sodium foods: Specialized low-sodium canned goods, proteins, and meal replacement systems
- Potassium control: Low-potassium food options and potassium monitoring guidelines
- Fluid management: Precise fluid measuring and intake tracking systems
- Medication support: Electrolyte monitoring and medication timing coordination
- Cost: $250-500 for renal diet, emergency food, and monitoring systems

Food Allergy Management

- EpiPen supplies: Multiple EpiPens with backup supplies and family training
- Allergen-free foods: Certified allergen-free food supplies with clear labeling
- Cross-contamination prevention: Separate cookware, storage, and preparation equipment
- Emergency medications: Antihistamines, corticosteroids, and emergency treatment protocols
- Cost: $300-600 for food allergy emergency management systems

Mental Health & Behavioral Considerations

Psychological Support Systems

Mental health conditions require continued support and medication management during emergencies when normal therapeutic support may be unavailable.

Medication Management

- Psychiatric medications: 14-day supply of all mental health medications with backup prescriptions
- Crisis medications: Anti-anxiety medications and emergency psychiatric intervention protocols
- Medication monitoring: Mood tracking and medication effectiveness assessment tools
- Professional contacts: 24-hour crisis hotlines and emergency psychiatric consultation services
- Cost: $100-300 for mental health medication and crisis support systems

Behavioral Support Systems

- Routine maintenance: Familiar items, activities, and routines that provide psychological stability
- Sensory support: Noise-canceling headphones, weighted blankets, and sensory regulation tools
- Communication aids: Picture cards, communication boards, and assistive communication devices
- Caregiver support: Respite care planning and caregiver stress management resources
- Cost: $150-400 for behavioral support and sensory regulation systems

Chapter Summary: Protecting Your Family's Most Vulnerable Members

Comprehensive special needs preparedness ensures that every family member receives appropriate care and support regardless of age, health status, or special requirements. By implementing the systems in this chapter, you'll have:

✓ **Complete infant and child support** with specialized nutrition, safety, and comfort systems

✓ **Senior care capability** addressing mobility, medication, and sensory support needs

✓ **Comprehensive pet preparedness** providing complete care for animal family members

✓ **Chronic disease management,** maintaining health for family members with ongoing medical conditions

✓ **Specialized dietary support** accommodating food allergies, restrictions, and medical diets

✓ **Mental health continuity** supporting psychological stability during high-stress emergencies

Implementation Priority Order:

1. Life-critical needs first: medications, infant formula, chronic disease supplies
2. Safety and mobility equipment for vulnerable family members
3. Comfort and psychological support items
4. Pet preparedness and animal family member needs
5. Educational and developmental support for children
6. Advanced monitoring and backup systems

Budget-Friendly Implementation Strategy:

- **Phase 1** (Month 1): Critical medical supplies and infant/senior basic needs ($400-800)
- **Phase 2** (Month 2): Pet supplies and specialized dietary requirements ($300-600)
- **Phase 3** (Month 3): Comfort items, educational materials, and advanced monitoring ($200-500)
- **Total Investment**: $900-1,900 for comprehensive special needs preparedness

Critical Success Factors:

- **Individual assessment**: Customize systems for each family member's specific needs

- **Backup redundancy**: Multiple supply sources and equipment backups for life-critical items
- **Training preparation**: Ensure all capable family members know how to provide specialized care
- **Regular updates**: Continuously adjust supplies as family members age and conditions change

Medical Preparedness Priorities:

- **Medication continuity**: Never allow prescription medications to run below a 7-day supply
- **Equipment reliability**: Backup power and redundant systems for life-critical medical equipment
- **Monitoring capability**: Track vital signs and health status during high-stress periods
- **Professional contact**: Maintain communication with healthcare providers and emergency services

Age-Appropriate Considerations:

- **Infants**: Complete nutritional and care independence with specialized safety equipment
- **Children**: Educational continuity, psychological support, and age-appropriate safety measures
- **Seniors**: Enhanced mobility support, complex medication management, and sensory assistance
- **Adults with disabilities**: Customized support maintaining independence and dignity

Pet Integration Benefits:

- **Family unity**: Pets provide psychological comfort and emotional stability during stress

- **Security benefits**: Dogs provide additional security awareness and protection capability
- **Responsibility maintenance**: Pet care provides routine and purpose during disrupted periods
- **Therapeutic value**: Animal companionship reduces stress and supports mental health

With specialized family needs addressed, we'll focus on security and self-defense systems that protect your family and preparedness investments from human threats during emergencies when normal law enforcement may be overwhelmed or unavailable.

Chapter 10

Security & Self-Defense

"Securing your home and equipping each family member with reliable defense tools reduces vulnerability and enhances peace of mind during emergencies when normal law enforcement may be overwhelmed or unavailable."

During major emergencies, normal security systems often fail while crime rates typically increase due to desperation, reduced law enforcement presence, and breakdown of social order. Your preparedness investments become targets, and your family becomes vulnerable without adequate protection systems. This chapter builds layered security and self-defense capabilities that deter threats, protect your family, and secure your preparedness resources through multiple defense levels.

10.1 Personal Defense & Non-Lethal Tools

Personal protection tools offer immediate defense capabilities that accompany family members and are effective in any location. Non-lethal options provide effective protection while minimizing legal complications and reducing the risk of weapons being used against family members.

Individual Protection Systems

Pepper Spray Defense Systems: Pepper spray provides effective personal protection with minimal training requirements and broad legal acceptance across jurisdictions.

Family Pepper Spray Collection

- Personal pepper spray: 4 canisters (one per adult and teen family member)
- Specifications: 2-4 million Scoville heat units, 10-to-15-foot effective range
- Spray pattern: Stream pattern for accuracy, cone pattern for multiple attackers
- Mounting systems: Belt holsters, keychain attachment, pocket clips for accessibility
- Cost: $15-25 each for quality pepper spray units

Pepper Spray Selection Criteria

- OC concentration: 10-18% oleoresin capsicum for maximum effectiveness
- UV marking dye: Identifies attackers for later police identification
- Safety features: Safety locks preventing accidental discharge during carry
- Expiration dating: Replace every 2-3 years to maintain effectiveness
- Practice canisters: Inert training sprays for safe practice and familiarity

Electronic Defense Tools
Personal Alarm Systems

High-decibel personal alarms attract attention and disorient attackers while summoning help from area residents or security personnel.

Personal Safety Alarms

- Quantity: 4 keychain-style personal alarms (130+ decibel output)
- Activation: Pull-pin activation that continues sounding until the pin is replaced

- Battery life: Long-life batteries with low-battery indicators
- Attachment: Keychain, belt clip, and lanyard options for secure carrying
- Cost: $10-20 each for quality personal safety alarms

Electronic Deterrent Devices

- Stun guns: 2 high-voltage stun guns for adults (verify local legality)
- TASER devices: 1-2 TASER units with cartridge reloads (law enforcement grade)
- Activation safety: Safety switches preventing accidental activation
- Training requirements: Professional training for effective and safe use
- Cost: $50-150 for stun guns, $300-500 for TASER devices

Impact & Striking Tools
Tactical Flashlights

Heavy-duty flashlights serve dual purposes as illumination tools and effective impact weapons while maintaining complete legal acceptance.

Tactical Flashlight Systems

- Quantity: 4 tactical flashlights (500+ lumen output, aircraft aluminum construction)
- Impact capability: Crenellated bezel for striking effectiveness
- Grip design: Anti-slip grip surfaces and lanyard attachment points
- Battery systems: Rechargeable batteries with backup alkaline capability
- Cost: $40-80 each for quality tactical flashlights

Defensive Tools & Training Aids

- Kubotan keychain: 4 tactical pens/kubotans for pressure point defense
- Self-defense keychains: Legal defensive tools designed for keychain carry
- Training equipment: Heavy bag, focus mitts for practice and skill development

- Instruction materials: Self-defense books, videos, and training guides
- Cost: $60-150 for a complete defensive tool and training system

10.2 Home Fortification & Security Devices

Home security systems transform your residence from a soft target to a hardened position that deters criminals and protects occupants. Layered security creates multiple barriers that delay intruders and provide early warning of security breaches.

Perimeter Security Systems

Exterior Lighting & Visibility Control

Lighting eliminates concealment opportunities for intruders while providing clear visibility for residents to identify threats and take appropriate action.

Motion-Activated Lighting

- Quantity: 4 motion-sensor flood lights covering all approach routes
- Power options: Solar-powered with battery backup, AC-powered with battery backup
- Coverage pattern: 180-degree detection pattern with 30 to 40-foot range
- Light output: 1000+ lumen LED output for effective area illumination
- Cost: $50-100 each for quality motion-activated security lighting

Perimeter Warning Systems

- Driveway alarms: Wireless sensors detecting vehicle and pedestrian approach
- Motion detectors: Battery-powered sensors covering property approaches
- Window/door alarms: Individual alarms for each potential entry point
- Wireless communication: Central monitoring system with multiple sensor integration

- Cost: $200-500 for a comprehensive perimeter detection system

Entry Point Reinforcement
Door Security Enhancement

Doors represent the primary entry points for most break-ins—proper reinforcement dramatically increases break-in difficulty and time requirements.

Door Frame Reinforcement Systems

- Strike plate reinforcement: Heavy-duty strike plates with 3-inch security screws
- Door jamb armor: Steel reinforcement plates preventing frame splitting
- Hinge reinforcement: Security hinges with non-removable pins
- Door thickness: Solid-core or steel doors replacing hollow-core doors
- Cost: $50-100 per door for comprehensive reinforcement

Advanced Door Security

- Deadbolt locks: Grade 1 ANSI deadbolts with 1-inch throw bolts
- Door security bars: Floor-to-door bracing systems preventing forced entry
- Peep holes: Wide-angle door viewers enabling visitor identification
- Door chains: Heavy-duty chain locks for controlled door opening
- Cost: $75-150 per door for advanced locking and security systems

Window Protection Systems
Window Security & Reinforcement

Windows are the most vulnerable entry points in most homes—proper protection eliminates easy access while maintaining emergency egress capability.

Security Window Film

- Coverage: 4 mil security film for all ground-floor and accessible

windows
- Installation: Professional installation ensuring proper adhesion and coverage
- Benefits: Holds glass together when broken, significantly delays entry attempts
- Appearance: Clear film maintains normal window appearance and light transmission
- Cost: $3-6 per square foot installed for security window film

Window Security Hardware

- Security bars: Removable security bars with quick-release mechanisms for emergency egress
- Window locks: Pin locks and keyed locks for double-hung and sliding windows
- Window sensors: Magnetic sensors detecting window opening or glass breaking
- Reinforcement: Laminated or tempered glass replacement for critical windows
- Cost: $30-80 per window for security hardware and reinforcement

Physical Barriers & Deterrents
Property Barrier Systems

- Fencing: 6-foot privacy fencing with anti-climb features
- Gates: Locking gates with reinforced hinges and strike plates
- Landscaping: Thorny shrubs and plants under windows, creating natural barriers
- Signage: Security system signs and warnings deterring casual criminals
- Cost: $15-30 per linear foot for fencing, $200-500 per gate

10.3 Fire Safety & Prevention

Fire represents one of the greatest threats to life and property during emergencies when fire departments may be overwhelmed or unable to respond. Comprehensive fire safety systems provide detection, suppression, and escape capability.

Fire Detection & Alarm Systems

Smoke & Fire Detection Early fire detection provides the time needed for suppression efforts or safe evacuation—detection systems must work during power outages and provide audible alerts throughout the home.

Advanced Smoke Detection Systems

- Smoke detectors: Battery-powered detectors for each bedroom, hallway, and living area
- Carbon monoxide detectors: CO detectors near bedrooms and fuel-burning appliances
- Heat detectors: Fixed-temperature detectors for areas where smoke detectors cause false alarms
- Interconnected systems: Wireless interconnection causes all alarms to sound when one is activated
- Cost: $25-50 per detector for quality battery-powered units

Fire Detection Maintenance

- Battery replacement: Monthly battery testing with annual battery replacement
- Detector testing: Weekly testing of all detectors using test buttons
- Cleaning schedule: Quarterly cleaning of detector sensors, preventing false alarms
- Replacement planning: 10-year detector replacement cycle, maintaining sensitivity
- Cost: $20-40 annually for batteries and maintenance supplies

Fire Suppression Equipment

Portable Fire Extinguishers Fire extinguishers provide immediate fire suppression capability for small fires before they become uncontrollable—proper selection and placement enable rapid response.

Fire Extinguisher Systems

- ABC-rated extinguishers: 2 extinguishers (5-10 lb. capacity) for kitchen and garage areas
- Mounting systems: Wall mounts, placing extinguishers in accessible locations
- Training: Family training on PASS technique (Pull, Aim, Squeeze, Sweep)
- Inspection schedule: Monthly pressure gauge checks and annual professional inspection
- Cost: $25-60 each for quality ABC fire extinguishers

Specialized Fire Suppression

- Fire blankets: 2 fire blankets for smothering small fires and protecting during evacuation
- Class K extinguisher: Kitchen-specific extinguisher for grease and cooking oil fires
- Automatic systems: Range hood suppression systems for kitchen fire protection
- Water supplies: Garden hoses and sprinkler systems for exterior fire suppression
- Cost: $100-300 for specialized fire suppression equipment

Emergency Escape Systems

Fire Escape Planning & Equipment Fire escape systems provide safe exit routes when primary exits become blocked by fire or smoke—escape equipment enables evacuation from upper floors.

Emergency Escape Ladders

- Portable ladders: 2 emergency escape ladders for second-story windows
- Window mounting: Secure mounting systems that deploy quickly during emergencies
- Capacity rating: Ladders rated for adult weight plus child carrying capability
- Storage: Compact storage near windows with easy access during emergencies
- Cost: $60-150 each for quality emergency escape ladders

Escape Route Planning

- Primary routes: Two escape routes from each room with clear pathway maintenance
- Meeting locations: Designated outdoor meeting locations for family accountability
- Practice schedule: Monthly escape drills with timing and route evaluation
- Emergency lighting: Battery-powered emergency lighting along escape routes
- Cost: $50-150 for emergency lighting and route marking systems

10.4 Training, Legal & Maintenance Considerations

Effective security and self-defense require ongoing training, legal compliance, and systematic maintenance to ensure systems work when needed and family members can use them effectively.

Self-Defense Training Systems

Family Self-Defense Education Self-defense skills require regular practice and proper instruction—training systems build confidence and capability while reducing injury risk during defense situations.

Professional Training Programs

- Self-defense classes: Enrollment in certified self-defense programs for

- all capable family members
- Martial arts training: Ongoing martial arts instruction, building physical and mental discipline
- Situational awareness: Training programs teaching threat recognition and avoidance
- De-escalation techniques: Communication skills, reducing the likelihood of physical confrontation
- Cost: $50-150 per person per month for quality self-defense training

Home Training Systems

- Training equipment: Heavy bags, focus mitts, and training weapons for home practice
- Instructional materials: DVDs, books, and online training resources
- Practice schedules: Regular family training sessions, maintaining skill levels
- Scenario training: Role-playing exercises, preparing for various threat situations
- Cost: $200-500 for home training equipment and instructional materials

Legal Compliance & Documentation

Security & Self-Defense Legal Requirements Security measures and self-defense tools must comply with local, state, and federal laws—legal violations can result in criminal charges even when defending family and property.

Legal Research & Compliance

- Local ordinances: Research city and county regulations on security devices and weapons
- State laws: Understanding state laws regarding self-defense, weapons, and property protection
- Federal regulations: Compliance with federal laws on weapons, surveil-

lance, and security devices
- Legal consultation: Annual consultation with an attorney specializing in self-defense law
- Cost: $200-500 for legal consultation and research

Documentation Systems

- Purchase records: Documentation of all security equipment and weapon purchases
- Training certificates: Records of training completion and skill certification
- Insurance coverage: Liability insurance covering security systems and self-defense actions
- Legal updates: Subscription services providing updates on relevant law changes
- Cost: $100-300 annually for documentation and legal update services

Maintenance & Testing Protocols
Security System Maintenance
Security equipment requires regular maintenance and testing to ensure proper function during emergencies—failed security systems provide false confidence and leave families vulnerable.
Equipment Testing Schedules

- Weekly testing: Security alarms, motion detectors, and communication systems
- Monthly testing: Fire extinguishers, emergency lighting, and escape equipment
- Quarterly testing: Window and door reinforcement, locks, and barrier systems
- Annual testing: Professional inspection of security systems and fire suppression equipment
- Cost: $200-500 annually for professional inspections and maintenance

Equipment Replacement Planning

- Battery replacement: Systematic battery replacement prevents system failures
- Equipment lifecycle: Replacement schedules for security equipment reaching end-of-service life
- Technology upgrades: Periodic upgrade of security technology, maintaining effectiveness
- Inventory management: Spare parts and backup equipment ensure continuous operation
- Cost: $300-800 annually for equipment replacement and upgrades

Family Security Protocols
Security Procedures & Communication
Effective security requires coordinated family procedures and clear communication protocols—security systems are only effective when family members know how to use them properly.

Daily Security Procedures

- Perimeter checks: Daily inspection of property security and potential vulnerabilities
- System activation: Consistent activation of security systems during absence and sleep periods
- Communication protocols: Check-in procedures when family members are away from home
- Threat assessment: Regular evaluation of local crime trends and security threats
- Cost: Time investment in training and procedure development

Emergency Response Procedures

- Threat response: Specific procedures for different types of security threats

- Communication plans: Emergency communication with law enforcement and family members
- Safe room procedures: Defensive positions and communication systems for home invasion scenarios
- Evacuation procedures: Security considerations during emergency evacuation
- Cost: Training time investment and emergency communication equipment

Community Security Integration
Neighborhood Watch & Mutual Aid

Community security multiplies individual family security through shared vigilance, mutual assistance, and coordinated response to threats.

Community Security Programs

- Neighborhood watch: Participation in organized neighborhood surveillance programs
- Communication networks: Radio networks and phone trees for security information sharing
- Mutual assistance: Agreements with neighbors for security assistance and resource sharing
- Training coordination: Group training programs reduce individual training costs
- Cost: $50-200 for communication equipment and group training participation

Professional Security Services

- Security consultations: Professional security assessments and recommendations
- Alarm monitoring: Professional monitoring services for security and fire alarm systems
- Private security: Security patrol services during extended emergencies

- Technology integration: Professional installation and maintenance of security systems
- Cost: $50-200 monthly for professional security services

Chapter Summary: Building Your Family's Security & Defense Capability

Comprehensive security and self-defense systems provide multiple layers of protection that deter threats, delay intruders, and enable effective family defense when normal law enforcement is unavailable. By implementing the systems in this chapter, you'll have:

✓ **Personal protection capability** with non-lethal tools and training for every family member

✓ **Hardened home security** through reinforcement, barriers, and detection systems

✓ **Fire safety systems** providing detection, suppression, and escape capability

✓ **Professional training** builds confidence and competence in security and self-defense

✓ **Legal compliance,** ensuring all security measures meet local and state requirements

✓ **Community integration** multiplying security through neighborhood cooperation and mutual aid

Implementation Priority Order:

1. Personal protection tools (pepper spray, tactical flashlights, personal alarms)
2. Basic home security (door reinforcement, window protection, lighting)
3. Fire safety systems (smoke detectors, fire extinguishers, escape planning)
4. Self-defense training and family security procedures
5. Advanced security systems (perimeter detection, surveillance, barriers)
6. Community security integration and professional services

Budget-Friendly Implementation Strategy:

- **Phase 1** (Month 1): Personal protection tools and basic door security ($200-400)
- **Phase 2** (Month 2): Fire safety systems and window protection ($300-600)
- **Phase 3** (Month 3): Advanced security systems and training programs ($400-800)
- **Total Investment**: $900-1,800 for a comprehensive family security capability

Legal Compliance Priorities:

- **Research requirements**: Understand local laws before purchasing security equipment
- **Training documentation**: Maintain records of security and self-defense training
- **Insurance coverage**: Ensure liability coverage for security systems and self-defense actions
- **Professional consultation**: Annual legal review of security measures and procedures

Training & Skill Development:

- **Professional instruction**: Quality training from certified instructors in self-defense and security
- **Regular practice**: Ongoing skill maintenance through training and practice
- **Family coordination**: Ensure all family members understand security procedures
- **Scenario training**: Practice response to various threat situations

Security System Integration:

- **Layered defense**: Multiple security measures working together
- **Redundancy**: Backup systems prevent single points of failure
- **Early warning**: Detection systems providing time for response and defense
- **Communication**: Family and community communication during security incidents

Maintenance & Reliability:

- **Regular testing**: Systematic testing ensures equipment functions when needed
- **Professional inspection**: Annual professional assessment of security systems
- **Equipment replacement**: Proactive replacement to prevent system failures
- **Technology updates**: Periodic upgrades maintain security effectiveness

Community Benefits:

- **Shared vigilance**: Neighborhood watch programs providing collective security
- **Resource sharing**: Community cooperation reduces individual security costs
- **Mutual assistance**: Neighbor support during security incidents and emergencies
- **Information sharing**: Communication networks providing threat awareness and coordination

With security and protection systems in place, we'll now focus on transportation and evacuation systems that enable safe, reliable mobility during your family's quick relocation or when regular transportation options are

CHAPTER 10

unavailable.

Chapter 11

Transportation & Evacuation

"Ensuring reliable transport and clear evacuation plans protects your family when you need to relocate quickly and maintains your primary evacuation asset when professional rescue services become unavailable."

Transportation becomes your lifeline during emergencies, allowing evacuation from danger zones, access to supplies and services, and relocation to safe areas. Vehicle breakdowns during evacuation can turn manageable emergencies into life-threatening situations. This chapter develops comprehensive transportation systems that maintain mobility regardless of fuel, road conditions, or mechanical issues while ensuring your family can evacuate quickly with essential supplies.

11.1 Vehicle Preparedness & Maintenance

Your primary vehicle represents your most important evacuation asset—proper maintenance, emergency equipment, and backup systems ensure transportation reliability when your family's safety depends on mobility.

Primary Vehicle Optimization

Vehicle Selection & Configuration Emergency-capable vehicles balance reliability, cargo capacity, fuel efficiency, and all-weather capability while

maintaining daily usability and reasonable operating costs.
Emergency Vehicle Characteristics

- Reliability record: Vehicles with documented long-term reliability and parts availability
- Ground clearance: Adequate clearance for debris, flood water, and poor road conditions
- Cargo capacity: Space for family plus 72-hour emergency supplies and evacuation equipment
- Fuel efficiency: Extended range capability, reducing refueling requirements during evacuation
- All-weather capability: 4WD or AWD for snow, mud, and adverse weather conditions

Vehicle Modification & Enhancement

- Roof cargo system: Roof rack or cargo box providing additional storage capacity
- Trailer hitch: Class III hitch enabling cargo trailer or small RV towing
- Emergency equipment mounting: Secure mounting for emergency tools and supplies
- Communication equipment: CB radio or HAM radio installation for emergency communication
- Cost: $500-2,000 for vehicle modifications and emergency equipment integration

Emergency Vehicle Equipment
Roadside Emergency & Repair Systems
Vehicle emergency equipment provides self-rescue capability and basic repair functionality when professional roadside assistance is unavailable.
Jump Starting & Electrical Systems

- Jumper cables: Heavy-duty 20-foot cables (4-gauge wire minimum) for

safe jump starting
- Portable jump starter: Lithium-ion battery pack with 12V output and USB charging ports
- Multimeter: Digital meter for electrical system diagnosis and battery testing
- Electrical repair kit: Wire, connectors, fuses, and electrical tape for field repairs
- Cost: $150-300 for a complete electrical emergency and repair system

Tire Repair & Inflation Systems

- Tire repair kit: Plug and patch kit for puncture repairs with tire irons
- Portable air compressor: 12V or battery-powered compressor with pressure gauge
- Tire pressure gauge: Accurate gauge (±1 PSI) for proper tire pressure maintenance
- Emergency tire sealant: Temporary tire sealant for sidewall damage and large punctures
- Cost: $100-200 for a comprehensive tire emergency repair system

Fuel Management & Storage

Fuel Security & Range Extension Fuel availability becomes unreliable during widespread emergencies—strategic fuel management ensures transportation capability when gas stations are closed or have long lines.

Fuel Storage Systems

- Portable fuel containers: 2 DOT-approved 5-gallon gas cans with spouts and funnels
- Fuel stabilizer: Treats 40 gallons of gasoline for 12 to 24 months of storage
- Fuel rotation system: Use and replace stored fuel every 6-12 months
- Secure storage: Ventilated outdoor storage away from ignition sources and living areas

- Cost: $60-120 for fuel storage containers and additives

Fuel Conservation & Efficiency

- Maintenance schedule: Regular tune-ups maintain optimal fuel efficiency
- Tire pressure monitoring: Proper inflation improves fuel economy by 3-5%
- Route planning: GPS systems with fuel-efficient routing and station location
- Driving techniques: Fuel-efficient driving practices extend range during evacuation
- Cost: Maintenance investment plus operational technique training

Vehicle Recovery & Extraction
Self-Recovery Equipment
Vehicle recovery systems enable extraction from mud, snow, sand, or debris without waiting for professional tow services.
Towing & Recovery Systems

- Tow strap: Heavy-duty 20-foot strap rated for 2× vehicle weight with reinforced loops
- Recovery shackles: Rated D-rings and clevis pins for secure attachment points
- Come-along winch: Manual cable winch (2 to 3-ton capacity) with 20 feet of steel cable
- Tree protection straps: Wide straps prevent bark damage during winch anchoring
- Cost: $150-300 for a manual vehicle recovery system

Traction & Mobility Aids

- Traction aids: Sand, kitty litter, or traction mats for wheel grip in

snow/mud
- Tire chains: Snow chains appropriately sized for vehicle tires
- Shovel: Folding military-style shovel for digging out stuck vehicles
- Recovery boards: Lightweight traction boards for sand, mud, and snow recovery
- Cost: $100-250 for traction and mobility assistance equipment

11.2 Evacuation Planning & Route Management

Effective evacuation requires pre-planned routes, alternative pathways, and decision-making criteria that enable rapid departure before escape routes become congested or blocked.

Route Planning & Navigation

Primary & Alternate Route Systems Evacuation routes must account for traffic congestion, road damage, fuel availability, and changing conditions during widespread emergencies.

Route Selection Criteria

- Multiple directions: Routes leading to different geographic areas and destinations
- Road capacity: Major highways for speed, back roads for avoiding congestion
- Fuel availability: Gas stations along routes with backup fuel stop options
- Emergency services: Hospitals, fire stations, and emergency shelters along routes
- Geographic barriers: Avoiding flood zones, fire-prone areas, and single-bridge chokepoints

Navigation & Communication Systems

- Paper maps: Current road maps covering a 200-mile radius from the home location

- GPS systems: Multiple GPS units with offline map capability and traffic updates
- Route marking: Highlighted maps with primary and alternate routes clearly marked
- Communication plan: Ham radio frequencies and cell phone backup for route updates
- Cost: $100-250 for navigation equipment and mapping systems

Decision Making & Triggers

Evacuation Decision Matrix: Clear decision-making criteria prevent dangerous delays while avoiding unnecessary evacuation that wastes resources and creates family disruption.

Evacuation Trigger Events

- Official evacuation orders: Government evacuation orders for your area
- Utility failures: Extended power, water, or gas service interruptions
- Transportation disruption: Road closures limiting evacuation route options
- Security concerns: Civil unrest, looting, or personal security threats in the area
- Environmental hazards: Wildfire, flood, chemical release, or other immediate dangers

Go/No-Go Decision Timeline

- Level 1 Alert: Prepare for possible evacuation, monitor conditions
- Level 2 Warning: Load vehicles, prepare family, monitor official communications
- Level 3 Order: Execute evacuation immediately, follow the primary route
- Emergency evacuation: Leave immediately with grab-and-go supplies only

- Decision documentation: Written criteria preventing emotional decision-making during stress

Family Coordination & Communication
Evacuation Coordination Systems

Family coordination ensures everyone knows their role, location, and responsibilities during time-critical evacuation situations.

Family Responsibility Matrix

- Adult responsibilities: Vehicle preparation, route selection, communication coordination
- Teen responsibilities: Assist with loading, pet care, and sibling supervision
- Child responsibilities: Personal items, comfort objects, following instructions
- Meeting locations: Primary and secondary meeting points if the family becomes separated
- Cost: Planning time investment and communication equipment

External Communication Plans

- Out-of-area contact: Designated contact person outside your geographic region
- Check-in procedures: Regular communication schedule with family and emergency contacts
- Social media: Facebook, Twitter updates for extended family and friend networks
- Emergency services: Communication procedures with local emergency management
- Cost: Communication equipment plus service charges for enhanced communication

11.3 Alternative Transportation Systems

When primary vehicles become unavailable, alternative transportation systems maintain family mobility and provide backup evacuation capability.

Bicycle Transportation Systems

Family Bicycle Preparedness Bicycles provide fuel-independent transportation that works when roads are congested, fuel is unavailable, or vehicles become inoperable.

Family Bicycle Fleet

- Adult bicycles: 2 multi-speed bikes suitable for carrying cargo and passengers
- Child bicycles: 2 age-appropriate bikes with safety equipment and training
- Bicycle trailers: Child-carrying trailer and cargo trailer for equipment transport
- Maintenance kit: Tools, spare parts, and repair supplies for field maintenance
- Cost: $800-2,000 for a complete family bicycle transportation system

Bicycle Safety & Equipment

- Safety equipment: Helmets, reflective clothing, and lights for visibility and protection
- Security systems: Locks and cables preventing theft during stops
- Cargo systems: Panniers, baskets, and bungee cords for equipment transport
- Weather protection: Rain gear and cold-weather clothing for adverse conditions
- Cost: $200-500 for bicycle safety and cargo equipment

Public & Alternative Transportation

Public Transportation Preparedness Understanding and preparing for public transportation options provides evacuation alternatives when personal vehicles are unavailable.

Public Transit Systems

- Route knowledge: Bus, train, and subway routes from your area to safe destinations
- Payment systems: Cash, transit cards, and payment options for public transportation
- Schedule information: Current schedules and emergency service modifications
- Accessibility: Wheelchair, stroller, and cargo limitations on public transport
- Cost: Transit fare cards and emergency cash for public transportation

Alternative Transportation Options

- Rideshare services: Uber, Lyft, and local rideshare applications with payment setup
- Taxi services: Local taxi company contact information and payment arrangements
- Emergency transportation: Medical transport and emergency evacuation services
- Community resources: Neighbor networks and community transportation sharing
- Cost: Service fees plus emergency transportation fund

Pedestrian Evacuation Systems

Walking & Hiking Preparedness Pedestrian evacuation may become necessary when all vehicle transportation becomes unavailable—walking systems enable long-distance foot travel with essential supplies.

Pedestrian Equipment & Supplies

- Backpacks: Quality hiking backpacks for each family member with

proper fit
- Walking shoes: Broken-in hiking boots or athletic shoes with extra socks
- Weather protection: Rain gear, cold weather clothing, sun protection
- Navigation tools: Compass, maps, and GPS devices for pedestrian navigation
- Cost: $400-800 for family pedestrian evacuation equipment

Long-Distance Walking Preparation

- Physical conditioning: Regular walking and hiking to build endurance
- Route planning: Walking routes with rest stops, water sources, and shelter options
- Supply caches: Pre-positioned supply caches along potential walking routes
- Communication plans: Check-in procedures during long-distance foot travel
- Cost: Time investment in physical preparation and route planning

11.4 Evacuation Supply Systems

Evacuation supplies must balance completeness with portability—strategic supply systems ensure your family has essential resources without overloading vehicles or limiting mobility.

Grab-and-Go Bag Systems

Individual Emergency Bags Personal emergency bags provide each family member with essential survival supplies that can be grabbed quickly during an emergency evacuation.

Adult Go-Bag Contents

- Clothing: 3-day supply of weather-appropriate clothing, including underwear and socks
- Personal items: Medications, eyeglasses, personal hygiene items,

identification documents
- Food & water: High-energy food bars, water purification tablets, collapsible water container
- Tools & equipment: Multi-tool, flashlight, emergency radio, batteries, cash
- Cost: $150-300 per adult for a complete grab-and-go bag

Child Go-Bag Modifications

- Comfort items: Favorite toy, blanket, or comfort object for psychological security
- Child-specific supplies: Diapers, formula, age-appropriate food, medications
- Entertainment: Books, games, or electronic devices with headphones
- Identification: ID bracelet, recent photo, emergency contact information
- Cost: $100-250 per child, depending on age and specific needs

Vehicle Emergency Supply Caches
Permanent Vehicle Supply Systems

Vehicle-based emergency supplies provide extended survival capability and support for stranded or delayed evacuation situations.

Vehicle Emergency Kit Components

- Shelter: Emergency blankets, tarp, rope for temporary shelter construction
- Food & water: 72-hour food supply, water storage, water purification capability
- Tools: Multi-tool, duct tape, zip ties, emergency repair supplies
- Communication: Two-way radios, cell phone chargers, emergency contact information
- Cost: $200-400 for a comprehensive vehicle emergency supply system

Seasonal Equipment Rotation

- Winter supplies: Extra blankets, warm clothing, ice scraper, sand/salt for traction
- Summer supplies: Sun protection, extra water, cooling towels, electrolyte supplements
- Regional hazards: Earthquake supplies, hurricane supplies, wildfire masks as appropriate
- Equipment inspection: Quarterly inspection and replacement of expired or damaged supplies
- Cost: $100-200 for seasonal equipment plus ongoing maintenance

Evacuation Logistics & Timing
Loading & Departure Procedures

Efficient evacuation procedures ensure rapid departure with essential supplies while preventing dangerous delays or forgotten critical items.

Pre-Positioned Loading Systems

- Loading lists: Laminated checklists for each family member's loading responsibilities
- Supply staging: Pre-positioned supplies in garage or designated loading area
- Vehicle preparation: Fuel level maintenance, emergency equipment checking
- Family roles: Assigned responsibilities preventing confusion during high-stress loading
- Cost: Organization time investment plus staging equipment

Departure Timeline Management

- 15-minute evacuation: Grab-and-go bags only, immediate departure
- 1-hour evacuation: Essential supplies, important documents, basic comfort items

- 4-hour evacuation: Extended supplies, valuable items, comprehensive preparation
- Planned relocation: Full preparation with non-essential items and comfort supplies
- Practice schedules: Regular evacuation drills with timing and efficiency evaluation

Destination Planning & Resource Management

Safe Destination Selection Evacuation destinations must provide safety, resources, and communication capability while remaining accessible during various emergency scenarios.

Destination Categories & Criteria

- Family/friends: Relatives and friends in different geographic areas willing to provide shelter
- Commercial lodging: Hotels, motels, and extended-stay facilities along evacuation routes
- Public shelters: Government emergency shelters, community centers, schools
- Camping/outdoor: State parks, campgrounds, and outdoor evacuation options
- Cost: Lodging expenses plus communication and coordination costs

Destination Resource Requirements

- Communication: Phone, internet, and emergency communication capability at the destination
- Medical access: Healthcare facilities and medication refill capability near the destination
- Supply access: Grocery stores, pharmacies, and emergency supply availability
- Pet accommodation: Pet-friendly lodging and veterinary services for animal family members

- Cost: Destination expenses plus resource access and pet accommodation fees

Chapter Summary: Building Your Family's Transportation & Evacuation Capability

Comprehensive transportation and evacuation systems ensure your family can relocate safely and efficiently when staying becomes more dangerous than leaving. By implementing the systems in this chapter, you'll have:

✓ **Reliable primary vehicle** with emergency equipment and maintenance systems

✓ **Strategic fuel management,** ensuring transportation capability when fuel becomes scarce

✓ **Alternative transportation,** including bicycles, public transit, and pedestrian options

✓ **Pre-planned evacuation routes** with alternatives and decision-making criteria

✓ **Complete evacuation supplies** balanced between completeness and portability

✓ **Destination planning** with multiple safe relocation options

Implementation Priority Order:

1. Primary vehicle emergency equipment and fuel storage systems
2. Evacuation route planning and navigation equipment
3. Grab-and-go bags and personal evacuation supplies
4. Alternative transportation systems (bicycles, pedestrian equipment)
5. Destination planning and advanced evacuation logistics
6. Vehicle recovery equipment and advanced mobility systems

Budget-Friendly Implementation Strategy:

- **Phase 1** (Month 1): Basic vehicle emergency equipment and fuel storage ($300-600)

- **Phase 2** (Month 2): Grab-and-go bags and navigation systems ($400-800)
- **Phase 3** (Month 3): Alternative transportation and advanced systems ($600-1,200)
- **Total Investment**: $1,300-2,600 for comprehensive transportation and evacuation capability

Vehicle Preparedness Priorities:

- **Reliability maintenance**: Regular service ensuring vehicle dependability during emergencies
- **Emergency equipment**: Tools and supplies for self-rescue and basic repairs
- **Fuel security**: Stored fuel and conservation practices extending operational range
- **Recovery capability**: Equipment for vehicle extraction and mobility restoration

Evacuation Planning Benefits:

- **Rapid departure**: Pre-planning enables quick evacuation without dangerous delays
- **Route flexibility**: Multiple route options prevent getting trapped by congestion or closures
- **Supply preparedness**: Evacuation supplies provide survival capability during displacement
- **Destination security**: Pre-arranged destinations ensure safe relocation options

Alternative Transportation Value:

- **Fuel independence**: Bicycles and pedestrian systems work without fuel availability

- **Congestion avoidance**: Alternative transport works when roads become impassable
- **Economic efficiency**: Lower-cost transportation options during extended emergencies
- **Physical fitness**: Alternative transportation maintains physical conditioning

Family Coordination Systems:

- **Clear responsibilities**: Everyone knows their evacuation role and responsibilities
- **Communication plans**: Procedures for staying in contact during separation
- **Practice schedules**: Regular drills, maintaining evacuation readiness, and efficiency
- **Decision criteria**: Objective triggers preventing dangerous evacuation delays

Supply Management Strategy:

- **Staged loading**: Different supply levels for different evacuation timeline scenarios
- **Weight management**: Balanced completeness with vehicle capacity and mobility
- **Personal responsibility**: The Individual supplies reduce family coordination complexity
- **Seasonal adjustment**: Equipment rotation matching seasonal hazards and conditions

Integration with Overall Preparedness:

- Transportation systems enable access to cached supplies and resources
- Evacuation capabilities protect preparedness investments through

relocation
- Vehicle systems provide mobile communication and power generation platforms
- Alternative transportation supports community mutual aid and resource sharing

With transportation and evacuation systems ensuring your family's mobility, we'll focus on planning, skills development, and family coordination systems that transform individual preparedness components into an integrated, practiced, and continuously improving family resilience system.

Chapter 12

Planning, Skills & Community Building

"A solid plan, practiced skills, and regular drills turn supplies into real preparedness, while community connections multiply your family's resilience through shared knowledge, resources, and mutual support."

Equipment and supplies are only the foundation of preparedness—true resilience comes from coordinated planning, practiced skills, and community relationships that transform individual preparation into collective strength. This final chapter builds the human systems that make all your preparedness investments effective: family coordination plans, essential skills development, regular practice schedules, and neighborhood networks that multiply your security and capabilities through mutual aid and shared resources.

12.1 Family Emergency Planning & Documentation

Comprehensive family planning creates the decision-making frameworks and coordination systems that enable effective emergency response when stress, time pressure, and changing conditions challenge normal family communication and coordination.

Family Emergency Plan Development

Core Family Planning Documents. Emergency plans must be simple enough to follow under stress while comprehensive enough to address the decisions and coordination challenges that arise during actual emergencies.

Family Emergency Plan Binder

- Family information: Contact information, medical data, and decision-making authority for all family members
- Emergency contacts: Local and out-of-area contacts with relationship and contact method details
- Evacuation plans: Routes, destinations, meeting points, and decision criteria with maps and directions
- Shelter-in-place procedures: Home defense, utility shutoff, communication, and supply management protocols
- Cost: $50-100 for binder, printing, lamination, and documentation supplies

Individual Responsibility Matrices

- Adult responsibilities: Leadership roles, decision-making authority, and specialized task assignments
- Teen responsibilities: Support roles, sibling care, technical tasks, and communication duties
- Child responsibilities: Personal care, following instructions, and age-appropriate emergency tasks
- Special needs coordination: Care responsibilities for family members requiring additional assistance
- Backup assignments: Secondary role assignments when primary responsible person is unavailable

Communication & Coordination Systems
Family Communication Networks

Communication systems maintain family coordination when normal phone service becomes unreliable and family members may be separated

by work, school, or emergency circumstances.
Internal Family Communication

- Two-way radios: Family radio network with designated channels and communication schedules
- Communication protocols: Check-in times, emergency signals, and status reporting procedures
- Code words: Simple code system for common situations and status reports
- Written messages: Message boards and note systems for home-based communication
- Cost: $200-400 for family radio network and communication equipment

External Communication Networks

- Out-of-area contact: Designated person outside your geographic region for message coordination
- Emergency service contacts: Local police, fire, medical, and emergency management phone numbers
- Neighborhood network: Communication systems with nearby neighbors and community members
- Social media: Facebook, Twitter, and other platforms for extended family and friend updates
- Cost: Communication service fees plus emergency contact coordination

Meeting Points & Rendezvous Systems
Family Accountability Systems

Meeting point systems ensure family members can find each other when normal meeting locations become unavailable or when emergencies scatter family members across different locations.

Primary Meeting Locations

- Home base: Primary residence with backup entry methods and communication systems
- Neighborhood location: Local school, community center, or landmark within walking distance
- Community location: Public facility outside immediate neighborhood but within local area
- Regional location: Destination outside local area for major evacuations or widespread emergencies
- Cost: Location coordination and communication equipment for meeting points

Meeting Point Procedures

- Timeline management: How long to wait at each meeting point before moving to next location
- Information systems: Message boards or communication methods at each meeting point
- Resource coordination: Emergency supplies and equipment cached at meeting locations
- Decision authority: Who makes decisions about moving between meeting points
- Backup procedures: Alternative meeting arrangements when primary locations become unavailable

Document Management & Legal Continuity
Emergency Document Systems

Document management ensures family legal continuity and provides essential information access during emergencies when normal record systems may be unavailable.

Document Accessibility Systems

- Family information cards: Laminated cards with essential information for each family member

- Emergency procedures: Step-by-step instructions for emergency tasks and decisions
- Contact information: Complete contact lists for family, friends, services, and professionals
- Legal documents: Copies of identification, insurance, medical, and property documents
- Cost: $100-200 for document preparation, copying, and protective storage

Information Distribution

- Home copies: Complete document sets stored in a secure, accessible home location
- Vehicle copies: Abbreviated document sets in each family vehicle
- Off-site storage: Complete document sets stored at a secure off-site location
- Digital copies: Encrypted digital copies on mobile devices and cloud storage
- Family member copies: Individual family members carry personal information cards

12.2 Essential Skills Development & Training

Skills training transforms preparedness equipment into effective capability while building confidence and competence that enable effective decision-making during high-stress emergency situations.

Life Safety Skills Training

Medical & First Aid Competency Medical skills provide immediate life-saving capability and ongoing health maintenance when professional medical care becomes delayed or unavailable.

Family Medical Training Program

- CPR certification: All family members over 12 receive CPR and AED

training
- First aid certification: Basic and advanced first aid training through the Red Cross or equivalent
- Family-specific medical training: Training specific to family member medical conditions (diabetes, allergies, etc.)
- Medical equipment training: Competency with all family medical equipment and supplies
- Cost: $100-200 per person for comprehensive medical training and certification

Medical Skills Practice & Maintenance

- Monthly medical drills: Practice scenarios using family medical equipment and supplies
- Quarterly skill review: Formal review of medical procedures and equipment operation
- Annual recertification: Maintain current certification in CPR, first aid, and specialized skills
- Equipment familiarity: Regular practice with all medical monitoring and treatment equipment
- Cost: Ongoing certification fees plus practice time investment

Technical & Mechanical Skills

Equipment Operation & Maintenance Technical competency ensures family members can operate, maintain, and repair essential preparedness equipment when manufacturer support and professional repair services become unavailable.

Equipment Training Programs

- Power systems: Solar panels, generators, batteries, and electrical equipment operation
- Communication equipment: Radio operation, programming, and maintenance procedures

- Water systems: Filtration, purification, and storage system operation and maintenance
- Tool usage: Proper and safe use of hand tools, power tools, and specialized equipment
- Cost: $200-500 for technical training programs and equipment familiarization

Maintenance Skill Development

- Basic repair skills: Equipment troubleshooting, parts replacement, and field repair techniques
- Preventive maintenance: Systematic maintenance schedules and procedures for all family equipment
- Tool proficiency: Competent use of repair tools and diagnostic equipment
- Parts and supply management: Inventory control and replacement part acquisition
- Cost: Training time investment plus ongoing practice and skill development

Outdoor & Survival Skills

Environmental Competency: Outdoor skills provide the capability for evacuation scenarios, temporary outdoor living, and resource acquisition when normal shelter and supply systems become unavailable.

Outdoor Skills Training

- Navigation skills: Map and compass use, GPS operation, and dead reckoning techniques
- Shelter construction: Temporary shelter building using natural and emergency materials
- Fire building: Safe fire starting and management for cooking, warmth, and signaling
- Water acquisition: Natural water source identification, collection, and

field purification
- Cost: $300-600 for outdoor skills training courses and practice equipment

Food & Resource Skills

- Food preservation: Canning, dehydrating, smoking, and other food preservation techniques
- Gardening skills: Food production using available space and resources
- Foraging knowledge: Safe identification and use of local edible plants and resources
- Hunting/fishing: Legal and ethical resource acquisition where appropriate and legal
- Cost: $200-500 for food production and resource acquisition training

12.3 Regular Practice & Skill Maintenance

Systematic practice and skill maintenance ensure capabilities remain sharp and equipment stays functional through regular use and testing rather than deteriorating through neglect.

Family Drill & Exercise Programs

Emergency Response Drills Regular drills build muscle memory and decision-making capability that function effectively under the stress and time pressure of actual emergencies.

Monthly Emergency Drills

- Evacuation drills: Timed family evacuation with supply loading and departure procedures
- Shelter-in-place drills: Home security, utility management, and supply utilization practice
- Medical emergency drills: First aid scenarios with different family members as patients
- Communication drills: Emergency communication procedures and

equipment testing
- Cost: Time investment in drill planning and execution

Drill Documentation & Improvement

- Drill timing: Record evacuation times and identify bottlenecks or delays
- Equipment testing: Verify that all equipment functions properly during drill scenarios
- Skill assessment: Evaluate family member competency and identify training needs
- Procedure refinement: Modify plans and procedures based on drill experience and lessons learned
- Cost: Documentation materials and procedure modification time

Skills Practice & Maintenance

Ongoing Skill Development: Skills deteriorate without regular practice—systematic skill maintenance ensures capabilities remain effective when emergencies demand competent performance.

Skill Maintenance Schedules

- Weekly skills: Basic equipment operation, communication procedures, family coordination
- Monthly skills: Advanced equipment operation, medical procedures, technical maintenance
- Quarterly skills: Complex scenarios, advanced techniques, specialized equipment operation
- Annual skills: Comprehensive skill review, advanced training, certification maintenance
- Cost: Practice time investment plus periodic training and certification fees

Family Skills Development

- Age-appropriate training: Skills training matched to family member age, ability, and interest
- Progressive skill building: Advanced skills building on a basic competency foundation
- Cross-training: Multiple family members are competent in each essential skill area
- Teaching skills: Family members teach skills to each other and community members
- Cost: Training materials and time investment in family skill development

Equipment Testing & Maintenance
Systematic Equipment Verification

Regular equipment testing ensures all preparedness investments remain functional and ready for use rather than failing during emergencies when replacement is impossible.

Equipment Testing Schedules

- Weekly testing: Communication equipment, lighting, basic tools, and supplies
- Monthly testing: Power systems, water filtration, vehicles, and transportation equipment
- Quarterly testing: Generators, advanced equipment, storage systems, and backup supplies
- Annual testing: Complete system testing, professional inspections, and equipment replacement
- Cost: Testing time investment plus equipment maintenance and replacement costs

Maintenance Documentation

- Equipment logs: Testing records, maintenance performed, and replacement dates

- Performance tracking: Equipment performance trends and degradation identification
- Replacement planning: Equipment lifecycle planning and replacement scheduling
- Vendor relationships: Maintain relationships with equipment suppliers and service providers
- Cost: Documentation system and administrative time investment

12.4 Community Integration & Mutual Aid

Community preparedness networks multiply individual family preparedness through resource sharing, skill exchange, and mutual assistance that transform neighborhoods into resilient communities.

Neighborhood Preparedness Networks

Local Community Organization Neighborhood preparedness groups coordinate community resources, share knowledge, and provide mutual assistance during emergencies when individual families need support beyond their own capabilities.

Neighborhood Network Development

- Community assessment: Identify neighbor skills, resources, and preparedness levels
- Resource inventory: Community resource database including equipment, supplies, and expertise
- Communication systems: Neighborhood communication networks using radios, phone trees, and social media
- Meeting schedules: Regular community meetings for planning, training, and relationship building
- Cost: Communication equipment plus meeting coordination and administration time

Community Skill & Resource Sharing

- Skill exchange: Community members teaching skills to neighbors (medical, technical, outdoor)
- Equipment sharing: Coordinated sharing of expensive equipment (generators, tools, vehicles)
- Group purchasing: Bulk buying of supplies reduces individual costs and improves access
- Training coordination: Group training programs reduce costs and improve neighborhood competency
- Cost: Shared training costs plus equipment and resource sharing coordination

Mutual Aid Agreements
Formalized Community Support

Mutual aid agreements establish clear expectations and procedures for community assistance during emergencies while maintaining individual family preparedness and responsibility.

Mutual Aid Planning

- Resource agreements: Formal agreements for resource sharing during emergencies
- Skill agreements: Commitment to provide specialized skills and knowledge to community members
- Security cooperation: Neighborhood security coordination and mutual protection agreements
- Communication protocols: Community communication procedures and information sharing systems
- Cost: Agreement documentation plus coordination and communication systems

Community Emergency Procedures

- Community response plans: Neighborhood-level emergency response and coordination procedures

- Resource allocation: Procedures for fair and effective community resource distribution
- Decision-making authority: Community leadership and decision-making during emergencies
- Conflict resolution: Procedures for resolving resource and priority conflicts during stress
- Cost: Planning time investment plus community coordination equipment

Professional & Service Integration
External Resource Networks
Professional relationships and service provider networks extend community preparedness capability through access to specialized knowledge, equipment, and services.
Professional Network Development

- Healthcare providers: Relationships with doctors, nurses, and medical professionals
- Technical specialists: Electricians, mechanics, contractors, and technical experts
- Emergency services: Relationships with local police, fire, and emergency management personnel
- Service providers: Relationships with suppliers, contractors, and essential service providers
- Cost: Relationship development time plus occasional consultation fees

Community Service Integration

- Emergency services coordination: Integration with local emergency management and first responders
- Volunteer organization participation: Red Cross, Community Emergency Response Teams (CERT)
- Religious and community organizations: Church and community group

emergency preparedness integration
- Business community relationships: Local business preparedness coordination and mutual support
- Cost: Training programs plus volunteer time commitment

Regional Preparedness Integration
Broader Community Resilience

Regional preparedness networks provide resource access and mutual aid capability beyond the immediate neighborhood while maintaining local community focus and control.

Regional Network Participation

- County emergency management: Participation in official county emergency preparedness programs
- Regional preparedness groups: Participation in regional preparedness organizations and networks
- Amateur radio networks: HAM radio emergency communication networks and training programs
- Regional training programs: Access to advanced training and specialized preparedness education
- Cost: Training fees plus equipment and communication costs for regional network participation

Information & Intelligence Networks

- Weather and hazard monitoring: Regional weather and hazard information sharing networks
- Threat assessment: Community threat assessment and information sharing systems
- Resource tracking: Regional resource availability and sharing coordination
- Best practices sharing: Regional sharing of preparedness techniques and lessons learned

- Cost: Communication equipment plus information sharing system participation

Community Resilience Building
Long-Term Community Development

Community resilience building creates sustainable preparedness capability that improves over time through shared experience, accumulated resources, and strengthened relationships.

Community Preparedness Projects

- Community gardens: Neighborhood food production capability and resource sharing
- Tool libraries: Community tool and equipment sharing reduces individual investment requirements
- Skill banks: Community skill and knowledge databases with training coordination
- Community emergency shelters: Neighborhood shelter capability for extended emergencies
- Cost: Community project investment plus ongoing maintenance and coordination

Community Preparedness Education

- Community workshops: Regular education programs on preparedness topics and skills
- Children's preparedness programs: Age-appropriate preparedness education and skill development
- Community drills: Neighborhood-wide emergency drills and response exercises
- Preparedness mentoring: Experienced preppers mentoring new community members
- Cost: Education materials plus instructor time and community coordination

Chapter Summary: Transforming Preparation into True Resilience

Planning, skills, and community integration transform individual preparedness from supply accumulation into comprehensive family and community resilience. By implementing the systems in this chapter, you'll have:

✓ **Comprehensive family planning** with clear procedures, communication systems, and coordination protocols

✓ **Essential skills competency** enabling effective use of preparedness equipment and supplies

✓ **Regular practice systems,** maintaining family readiness through ongoing drills and skill development

✓ **Community integration,** multiplying family preparedness through neighborhood networks and mutual aid

✓ **Professional relationships,** providing access to specialized knowledge and emergency services

✓ **Continuous improvement** systems ensuring preparedness capability grows stronger over time

Implementation Priority Order:

1. Family emergency planning and communication systems
2. Essential skills training (medical, technical, outdoor)
3. Regular drill and practice schedules
4. Neighborhood network development and community integration
5. Professional relationship building and service integration
6. Advanced community resilience projects and long-term development

Budget-Friendly Implementation Strategy:

- **Phase 1** (Month 1): Family planning and basic skills training ($300-600)
- **Phase 2** (Month 2): Equipment training and community networking ($200-500)
- **Phase 3** (Month 3-6): Advanced skills, community projects, and professional integration ($400-1,000)

- **Total Investment**: $900-2,100 for comprehensive planning, skills, and community integration

Family Planning Benefits:

- **Coordinated response**: Clear procedures enabling effective family coordination during stress
- **Decision-making frameworks**: Objective criteria for emergency decisions, reducing confusion and delays
- **Communication continuity**: Multiple communication methods maintain family contact
- **Legal continuity**: Document systems ensuring family legal and financial continuity

Skills Development Value:

- **Equipment competency**: Ability to actually use preparedness equipment effectively
- **Confidence building**: Skills training reduces emergency stress and improves decision-making
- **Problem-solving capability**: Skills enable adaptation to changing emergency conditions
- **Teaching ability**: Competent family members can teach skills to others

Community Integration Benefits:

- **Resource multiplication**: Access to community resources and equipment beyond individual family capability
- **Knowledge sharing**: Community expertise covering areas where individual families lack knowledge
- **Mutual security**: Community cooperation providing security and assistance during emergencies
- **Cost sharing**: Community coordination reducing individual prepared-

ness costs

Practice & Maintenance Systems:

- **Skill preservation**: Regular practice preventing skill deterioration over time
- **Equipment reliability**: Regular testing ensuring equipment functions when needed
- **Procedure refinement**: Experience-based improvement of emergency procedures
- **Family readiness**: Ongoing readiness rather than one-time preparation

Long-Term Resilience Building:

- **Continuous improvement**: Systems that grow stronger through experience and practice
- **Adaptive capability**: Flexibility to adapt to changing conditions and new challenges
- **Community resilience**: Individual family preparedness contributing to broader community strength
- **Cultural integration**: Preparedness is becoming a normal part of family and community culture

Integration with All Previous Chapters:

- Planning systems coordinate all preparedness investments into a coherent capability
- Skills training enables the effective use of water, food, medical, and security systems
- Community integration multiplies the value of individual family preparedness investments
- Practice systems ensure all preparedness components work together

effectively

The Complete Preparedness System: Through the twelve chapters of this guide, you've built a comprehensive preparedness system that addresses every aspect of family resilience:

1. **Water security** (Chapter 1): 56 gallons stored plus purification capability
2. **Food independence** (Chapter 2): 14-day nutrition with cooking capability
3. **Medical preparedness** (Chapter 3): Complete healthcare capability
4. **Repair capability** (Chapter 4): Tools and materials for maintenance and fortification
5. **Power & communication** (Chapter 5): Energy independence and information access
6. **Shelter & warmth** (Chapter 6): Protection and comfort in any environment
7. **Hygiene & sanitation** (Chapter 7): Health maintenance and dignity preservation
8. **Documentation & finance** (Chapter 8): Legal continuity and resource access
9. **Special needs** (Chapter 9): Care for vulnerable family members and pets
10. **Security & defense** (Chapter 10): Protection from human and fire threats
11. **Transportation & evacuation** (Chapter 11): Mobility and relocation capability
12. **Planning & community** (Chapter 12): Coordination, skills, and mutual aid

Total Investment Summary:

- **Essential systems** (Chapters 1-8): $6,000-12,000 for basic family

preparedness
- **Advanced systems** (Chapters 9-12): $4,000-8,000 for comprehensive capability
- **Complete preparedness**: $10,000-20,000 for professional-grade family resilience

The Path Forward: True preparedness is never complete—it's an ongoing process of learning, practicing, improving, and adapting. Start with the most critical needs (water, food, medical), build systematically over time, and focus on developing skills and community relationships that multiply your preparedness investments. Most importantly, make preparedness a normal part of your family life rather than a burden or source of stress.

Your family's safety and resilience are worth the investment. The peace of mind that comes from true preparedness—knowing you can provide for your family's needs regardless of what challenges arise—is invaluable. Begin today, build systematically, practice regularly, and create the resilient, prepared family that can face any challenge with confidence and capability.

Chapter 13

Resource Optimization & Technology

"Advanced systems for inventory management, technology integration, and community coordination transform basic preparedness into a sophisticated, efficient, and continuously improving resilience network."

While the first twelve chapters built your foundational preparedness systems, true long-term resilience requires sophisticated resource management, technology integration, and optimization strategies that maximize efficiency, reduce waste, and enable continuous improvement. This chapter provides advanced systems that transform basic preparedness into a professional-grade operation using modern technology, systematic optimization, and strategic resource management.

13.1 Advanced Inventory Management Systems

Professional inventory management prevents waste, ensures freshness, optimizes storage space, and provides real-time visibility into resource availability—transforming preparedness from static stockpiling into dynamic resource management.

Digital Inventory Tracking
Comprehensive Database Systems

Modern inventory management uses digital systems that track quantities, expiration dates, locations, and usage patterns while providing automated alerts and reorder recommendations.

Inventory Management Software

- Database platform: Cloud-based inventory system accessible from multiple devices
- Barcode scanning: Mobile app with barcode scanning for rapid inventory updates
- Automated alerts: Expiration date warnings, low-stock alerts, and reorder notifications
- Location tracking: Multi-location inventory with precise storage location mapping
- Cost: $20-50 monthly for professional inventory management software

Digital Tracking Implementation

- Item cataloging: Complete digital catalog of all preparedness supplies with photos
- QR code labeling: Custom QR codes for instant mobile access to item information
- Batch tracking: Manufacturing dates, expiration dates, and supplier information
- Usage analytics: Consumption patterns and optimal reorder quantities
- Cost: $100-300 for initial setup, labeling equipment, and system configuration

Automated Rotation Systems

First-In-First-Out (FIFO) Management

Automated rotation systems ensure the oldest items are used first while maintaining optimal inventory levels without manual tracking or decision-making.

Physical Rotation Systems

- Gravity-fed dispensers: Automated dispensing systems for canned goods and packaged items
- Rotation shelving: Angled shelving systems that automatically move older items to the front
- Color-coded dating: Visual systems for quick identification of the oldest items
- Automated reminders: Calendar integration with rotation and replacement schedules
- Cost: $200-600 for automated physical rotation systems

Smart Storage Solutions

- Climate monitoring: Automated temperature and humidity monitoring with alerts
- Inventory sensors: Weight-based sensors that detect inventory levels automatically
- Smart locks: Electronic access control with usage logging and security monitoring
- Integration systems: Connecting physical storage with digital inventory management
- Cost: $300-800 for smart storage monitoring and control systems

Predictive Analytics & Optimization
Consumption Pattern Analysis
Advanced analytics identify usage patterns, optimize inventory levels, and predict future needs based on family consumption data and seasonal variations.
Analytics & Forecasting Systems

- Consumption tracking: Detailed analysis of family consumption patterns and seasonal variations
- Predictive modeling: Forecasting future needs based on historical usage and family changes

- Optimization algorithms: Automated calculation of optimal inventory levels and reorder points
- Scenario planning: "What-if" analysis for different emergency duration and intensity scenarios
- Cost: $50-200 for analytics software and data analysis tools

Cost Optimization Systems

- Price tracking: Monitoring supplier prices and identifying optimal purchase timing
- Bulk purchasing analysis: Calculating optimal quantity purchases, balancing cost and storage
- Supplier comparison: Automated comparison of suppliers for price, quality, and delivery
- Budget forecasting: Predictive budgeting for preparedness, maintenance, and expansion
- Cost: Price monitoring software $30-100 monthly, plus analysis time investment

13.2 Technology Integration & Automation

Modern technology enables sophisticated monitoring, control, and optimization of preparedness systems while providing remote access and automated management capability.

Smart Home Integration

Internet of Things (IoT) Integration

IoT devices provide continuous monitoring and control of preparedness systems while enabling remote management and automated responses to changing conditions.

Environmental Monitoring Systems

- Multi-sensor networks: Temperature, humidity, air quality, and light monitoring throughout the home

- Water quality monitoring: Continuous monitoring of water storage systems and purification equipment
- Power system monitoring: Real-time tracking of battery levels, solar production, and power consumption
- Security integration: Motion sensors, cameras, and access controls integrated with preparedness systems
- Cost: $500-1,500 for a comprehensive IoT monitoring network

Automated Control Systems

- Climate control: Automated heating, cooling, and ventilation for optimal storage conditions
- Irrigation systems: Automated watering for emergency food gardens and water storage maintenance
- Backup power switching: Automatic transfer switches for seamless backup power activation
- Security responses: Automated responses to security threats, including lighting, alerts, and communication
- Cost: $800-2,500 for automated control system installation and configuration

Mobile Technology Integration
Smartphone & Tablet Applications

Mobile technology provides instant access to preparedness information, enables remote monitoring, and supports field operations during emergencies.

Custom Preparedness Apps

- Inventory management: Mobile access to complete inventory with barcode scanning and updates
- Emergency procedures: Digital checklist and procedure access with offline capability
- Family communication: Secure family communication with location

sharing and status updates
- Resource mapping: Interactive maps showing resource locations, routes, and alternative options
- Cost: $100-500 for custom app development or premium preparedness app subscriptions

Offline Capability Systems

- Downloaded maps: Complete offline mapping for the local area, including roads, terrain, and resources
- Reference libraries: Offline access to technical manuals, medical references, and procedural guides
- Communication backup: Mesh networking apps enabling phone-to-phone communication without cellular
- Data synchronization: Automatic sync when connectivity is available, offline operation when not
- Cost: $50-200 for offline-capable apps and downloaded reference materials

Advanced Communication Networks
Professional Communication Systems

Advanced communication systems provide reliable, long-range communication capability that works when cellular and internet systems become overloaded or unavailable.

Amateur Radio Integration

- Digital modes: Packet radio, APRS, and digital messaging systems for data communication
- Repeater networks: Access to local and regional repeater systems for extended range
- Emergency networks: Integration with emergency communication networks and protocols
- Computer integration: Radio-to-computer interfaces for digital com-

munication and data logging
- Cost: $800-2,000 for advanced amateur radio systems and computer integration

Mesh Networking Systems

- Local mesh networks: Community-wide mesh networking for local communication without infrastructure
- Internet gateway: Mesh network internet access when some nodes have connectivity
- Voice and data: Combined voice, text, and data communication across a mesh network
- Mobile integration: Smartphone integration with mesh networking for seamless communication
- Cost: $300-800 for mesh networking equipment and community deployment

Data Management & Analytics
Information Systems & Decision Support

Advanced information systems provide decision support, trend analysis, and predictive capability that improve preparedness effectiveness and resource allocation.

Data Analytics Platforms

- Preparedness metrics: Tracking preparedness readiness levels and improvement trends
- Resource optimization: Analysis of resource utilization and optimization opportunities
- Community integration: Neighborhood resource sharing and mutual aid coordination systems
- Threat assessment: Integration with weather, news, and threat intelligence for proactive planning
- Cost: $100-400 for analytics platforms and data integration services

Knowledge Management Systems

- Document management: Centralized storage and access to all preparedness documents and procedures
- Lesson learned systems: Capturing and sharing experience from drills and actual emergencies
- Best practices database: Community sharing of effective preparedness techniques and solutions
- Training management: Tracking training completion, certification status, and skill development
- Cost: $50-300 for knowledge management platforms and content organization

13.3 Community Resource Networks

Advanced community integration creates resource networks that multiply individual preparedness through coordinated sharing, bulk purchasing, and mutual aid systems.

Neighborhood Resource Sharing
Community Resource Databases
Digital systems enable efficient sharing of resources, skills, and equipment across neighborhood networks while maintaining accountability and fair usage.

Shared Resource Management

- Equipment library: Community database of shareable equipment with reservation and tracking
- Skill directory: Neighborhood database of skills and expertise with availability and contact
- Supply coordination: Community coordination of bulk purchasing and resource sharing
- Service exchange: Bartering and service exchange systems using community credits or time banks

- Cost: $200-600 for the community resource management platform and administration

Community Purchasing Networks

- Bulk buying coordination: Organizing community bulk purchases for better pricing and access
- Group contracts: Community contracts with suppliers for priority access and emergency services
- Shared storage: Community storage facilities for bulk purchases and shared equipment
- Distribution systems: Fair distribution systems for community-purchased resources
- Cost: Community investment in shared purchasing and storage facilities

Regional Preparedness Networks
Multi-Community Integration

Regional networks provide access to resources, expertise, and mutual aid beyond the immediate neighborhood while maintaining local community control and priorities.

Regional Network Participation

- Resource sharing: Inter-community resource sharing agreements and coordination systems
- Information networks: Regional information sharing about threats, resources, and best practices
- Training coordination: Regional training programs and instructor sharing reduce costs
- Emergency coordination: Regional mutual aid agreements and emergency response coordination
- Cost: $100-500 for regional network participation and coordination systems

Professional Network Integration

- Healthcare networks: Regional healthcare provider networks for emergency medical consultation
- Technical expertise: Regional networks of technical specialists and professional consultants
- Supply chain integration: Regional supplier networks for priority access and emergency procurement
- Government liaison: Integration with regional emergency management and government services
- Cost: Professional consultation fees and network participation costs

Digital Community Platforms
Online Community Coordination

Digital platforms enable efficient community coordination, information sharing, and resource management while maintaining privacy and security.

Community Communication Platforms

- Secure messaging: Encrypted community communication platforms with role-based access
- Resource coordination: Digital coordination of community resources and mutual aid
- Information sharing: Community information sharing with verification and reliability scoring
- Event coordination: Community meeting, training, and exercise coordination systems
- Cost: $30-150 monthly for community platform hosting and administration

Community Resilience Metrics

- Preparedness assessment: Community-wide preparedness assessment and improvement tracking

- Resource mapping: Community resource mapping and gap analysis systems
- Vulnerability analysis: Community vulnerability assessment and mitigation planning
- Progress tracking: Community resilience improvement tracking and goal management
- Cost: Assessment tools and community coordination time investment

13.4 Advanced Optimization Strategies

Sophisticated optimization strategies maximize preparedness effectiveness while minimizing costs, storage requirements, and maintenance burden through strategic analysis and systematic improvement.

Multi-Use & Redundancy Optimization
Strategic Equipment Selection

Advanced equipment selection prioritizes multi-use capability, standardization, and strategic redundancy while avoiding unnecessary duplication and specialization.

Multi-Function Analysis

- Equipment capability mapping: Comprehensive analysis of equipment capabilities and overlap
- Consolidation opportunities: Identifying opportunities to reduce equipment inventory through multi-use items
- Standardization benefits: Analysis of standardization opportunities, reducing parts and maintenance complexity
- Strategic redundancy: Optimal redundancy levels balancing reliability with cost and storage requirements
- Cost: Analysis time investment plus strategic equipment replacement costs

Modular System Design

- Component compatibility: Designing systems with interchangeable and compatible components
- Scalable capability: Systems that can be expanded or contracted based on changing needs
- Maintenance optimization: Reducing maintenance complexity through standardization and modularity
- Upgrade pathways: Planning for technology upgrades and capability improvements over time
- Cost: System redesign and component standardization investment

Space & Storage Optimization
Advanced Storage Solutions

Sophisticated storage systems maximize storage efficiency while maintaining accessibility, organization, and environmental protection for preparedness supplies.

Vertical Storage Systems

- High-density shelving: Vertical storage systems maximize storage per square foot
- Automated retrieval: Mechanized storage and retrieval systems for frequently accessed items
- Climate-controlled storage: Optimized environmental control for different storage requirements
- Modular storage: Flexible storage systems that adapt to changing inventory requirements
- Cost: $1,000-5,000 for advanced storage system installation

Off-Site Storage Integration

- Distributed storage: Strategic placement of supplies across multiple secure locations
- Community storage: Participation in community storage facilities and resource sharing

- Commercial storage: Climate-controlled commercial storage for long-term supplies
- Mobile storage: Vehicle-based and portable storage systems for evacuation scenarios
- Cost: Storage facility costs plus transportation and coordination expenses

Economic Optimization & Financing
Financial Strategy & Resource Allocation

Advanced financial management optimizes preparedness investments while minimizing cost burden and maximizing return on preparedness investment.

Investment Strategy Optimization

- Cost-benefit analysis: Systematic analysis of preparedness investments and risk reduction value
- Financing strategies: Optimal financing approaches for large preparedness investments
- Insurance integration: Preparedness investments, reducing insurance costs and premiums
- Tax optimization: Tax-advantaged approaches to preparedness investment and expense management
- Cost: Financial planning consultation $300-800 plus ongoing management time

Community Investment Strategies

- Shared investment: Community investment in high-cost equipment and facilities
- Group purchasing: Leveraging community purchasing power for better pricing and access
- Investment recovery: Strategies for recovering preparedness investment through community services

- Economic resilience: Building community economic resilience and mutual aid systems
- Cost: Community coordination and investment management costs

Continuous Improvement Systems

Performance Measurement & Enhancement Systematic improvement processes ensure preparedness systems become more effective over time through measurement, analysis, and continuous refinement.

Metrics & Performance Tracking

- Preparedness metrics: Key performance indicators measuring preparedness effectiveness
- Improvement tracking: Systematic tracking of preparedness improvements and investments
- Benchmark comparison: Comparing preparedness levels against community and national standards
- Goal management: Setting and tracking preparedness goals and improvement targets
- Cost: Measurement system development and ongoing tracking time investment

Innovation & Adaptation

- Technology adoption: Systematic evaluation and adoption of new preparedness technologies
- Best practices integration: Continuous integration of new techniques and proven practices
- Lesson learned systems: Capturing and applying lessons from drills, exercises, and actual emergencies
- Community innovation: Sharing and adopting innovations developed by community members
- Cost: Innovation research and implementation costs plus community coordination time

CHAPTER 13

Chapter Summary: Building Advanced Preparedness Systems

Advanced resource optimization and technology integration transform basic preparedness into sophisticated, efficient, and continuously improving systems that maximize effectiveness while minimizing cost and complexity. By implementing the advanced systems in this chapter, you'll have:

✓ **Professional inventory management** with automated tracking, rotation, and optimization

✓ **Smart technology integration** providing monitoring, control, and remote access capability

✓ **Advanced communication systems** with digital modes, mesh networking, and professional capability

✓ **Community resource networks** multiply individual preparedness through coordinated sharing

✓ **Optimization strategies** maximizing effectiveness while minimizing cost and complexity

✓ **Continuous improvement systems,** ensuring preparedness capability, strengthen over time

Implementation Priority Order:

1. Digital inventory management and tracking systems
2. Basic smart home integration and environmental monitoring
3. Community resource sharing and coordination systems
4. Advanced communication and networking systems
5. Optimization analysis and system refinement
6. Continuous improvement and innovation systems

Budget-Friendly Implementation Strategy:

- **Phase 1** (Months 1-3): Digital inventory and basic smart systems ($500-1,500)
- **Phase 2** (Months 4-6): Community integration and communication systems ($800-2,000)
- **Phase 3** (Months 7-12): Advanced optimization and automation

systems ($1,200-4,000)
- **Total Investment**: $2,500-7,500 for advanced preparedness optimization systems

Technology Integration Benefits:

- **Automation**: Reducing manual management burden while improving accuracy and reliability
- **Remote access**: Monitoring and controlling systems from any location
- **Predictive capability**: Anticipating needs and problems before they become critical
- **Data-driven decisions**: Using analytics to optimize resource allocation and strategy

Community Network Value:

- **Resource multiplication**: Access to community resources beyond individual family capability
- **Cost reduction**: Shared investment reduces individual financial burden
- **Knowledge sharing**: Community expertise exceeding individual family knowledge
- **Mutual aid**: Community support during individual family emergencies

Advanced System Characteristics:

- **Scalable**: Systems that grow with family needs and community participation
- **Interoperable**: Components that work together rather than as isolated systems
- **Maintainable**: Systems designed for long-term operation with reasonable maintenance
- **Upgradeable**: Technology systems with clear upgrade paths and

compatibility

Optimization Strategy Results:

- **Efficiency gains**: Better results with less resource investment
- **Reduced complexity**: Simpler systems that are easier to operate and maintain
- **Improved reliability**: Multiple redundant systems prevent single points of failure
- **Lower long-term costs**: Strategic investment reduces ongoing operational expenses

Professional-Grade Capabilities:

This chapter transforms preparedness from an amateur hobby to a professional-grade capability:

- **Systematic management**: Professional inventory and resource management systems
- **Advanced communication**: Communication capability rivaling emergency services
- **Community integration**: Neighborhood resilience networks with sophisticated coordination
- **Continuous improvement**: Systems that become more capable over time through learning and optimization

Integration with Previous Chapters:

Advanced systems enhance all previous preparedness investments:

- **Inventory management** optimizes water, food, medical, and supply systems (Chapters 1-4)
- **Smart monitoring** enhances power, shelter, and sanitation systems (Chapters 5-7)
- **Digital documentation** improves document and financial systems

(Chapter 8)
- **Technology support** assists special needs and security systems (Chapters 9-10)
- **Communication networks** enhance transportation and community systems (Chapters 11-12)

The Evolution of Preparedness: This chapter represents the evolution from basic preparedness to advanced resilience:

- **Basic preparedness**: Having supplies and equipment
- **Intermediate preparedness**: Having skills and plans
- **Advanced preparedness**: Having optimized systems and community networks
- **Expert preparedness**: Having continuous improvement and innovation capability

Long-Term Value: Advanced systems provide compounding returns on preparedness investment:

- **Reduced waste**: Better inventory management prevents spoilage and obsolescence
- **Improved effectiveness**: Technology enabling better decision-making and resource allocation
- **Community benefits**: Shared systems reduce individual costs while improving capability
- **Futureproofing**: Systems designed to adapt and improve rather than become obsolete

This advanced chapter complements the foundational preparedness systems with sophisticated management, optimization, and technology integration that transforms good preparedness into exceptional resilience capability.

Chapter 14

Beyond Basic Preparedness

"Advanced resilience systems that go beyond survival to create sustainable, self-reliant communities capable of thriving during extended disruptions and building stronger foundations for long-term security."

While the previous chapters built comprehensive emergency preparedness, true long-term resilience requires systems that go beyond mere survival to establish sustainable, productive, and increasingly self-reliant communities. This final chapter examines advanced concepts such as renewable resource production, economic resilience, psychological preparedness, and community development that turn emergency preparedness into lasting lifestyle improvements and long-term security.

14.1 Advanced Power & Water Independence

Moving beyond emergency backup systems to create permanent infrastructure that reduces dependence on external utilities while providing superior reliability and long-term cost savings.

Comprehensive Renewable Energy Systems
Whole-Home Solar & Battery Integration
Advanced energy systems provide complete electrical independence with

grid-tie capability, battery backup, and load management that eliminates utility dependence while maintaining modern comfort levels.

Professional Solar Installation

- System sizing: 15-25 kW solar array providing 150% of annual household consumption
- Battery storage: 40-80 kWh lithium battery bank providing 3-7 days backup power
- Grid integration: Net metering with automatic grid disconnect during outages
- Load management: Smart electrical panel with priority load management during battery operation
- Cost: $35,000-75,000 for a complete whole-home renewable energy system

Advanced Energy Management

- Consumption monitoring: Real-time tracking of energy production, consumption, and storage
- Predictive management: Weather-based energy production forecasting and load scheduling
- Automated systems: Intelligent load shedding and battery management, optimizing system performance
- Remote monitoring: Cloud-based system monitoring with smartphone alerts and control
- Cost: $2,000-5,000 for advanced energy management and monitoring systems

Backup Generation Integration

- Hybrid systems: Solar/battery/generator integration providing multiple power sources
- Automatic switching: Seamless switching between solar, battery, and

generator power
- Fuel flexibility: Multi-fuel generators capable of running on propane, natural gas, gasoline, or diesel
- Exercise scheduling: Automated generator exercise and maintenance scheduling
- Cost: $5,000-15,000 for integrated backup generation systems

Water Independence & Production
Complete Water System Integration

Advanced water systems provide complete water independence through multiple sources, treatment, storage, and recycling that eliminate dependence on municipal water while ensuring superior quality.

Well Water & Pump Systems

- Deep well drilling: Artesian well providing a reliable water source independent of surface conditions
- Solar pump systems: Solar-powered well pumps with battery backup for continuous operation
- Water treatment: Multi-stage filtration and treatment providing superior water quality
- Storage integration: Well water feeding large-capacity storage systems with distribution pumps
- Cost: $8,000-25,000 for complete well drilling, pump, and treatment system

Rainwater Harvesting Systems

- Large-scale collection: Whole-roof rainwater collection with first-flush diverters
- Storage capacity: 5,000 to 10,000-gallon storage systems with multiple tank configurations
- Treatment systems: Filtration, UV sterilization, and chemical treatment for potable water

- Distribution systems: Pressurized distribution with automatic pump controls
- Cost: $10,000-30,000 for large-scale rainwater harvesting and treatment

Greywater & Blackwater Systems

- Greywater recycling: Treatment and reuse of laundry and shower water for irrigation
- Blackwater treatment: On-site sewage treatment with composting or constructed wetland systems
- Water recycling: Closed-loop water systems minimize water consumption and waste
- Irrigation integration: Treated water distribution for food production and landscaping
- Cost: $15,000-40,000 for complete wastewater treatment and recycling systems

Off-Grid Communication Networks
Long-Range Communication Independence
Professional communication systems provide reliable long-distance communication independent of cellular, internet, and telephone infrastructure.
Amateur Radio Infrastructure

- Base station setup: High-power amateur radio with tower, antennas, and backup power
- Digital communication: Packet radio, APRS, and digital modes for data communication
- Repeater access: Local repeater ownership or membership providing community communication
- Emergency networks: Integration with regional and national emergency communication networks
- Cost: $5,000-15,000 for professional amateur radio base station and

infrastructure

Satellite Communication Systems

- Voice/data service: Satellite phone and data service for global communication capability
- Internet access: Satellite internet providing broadband access independent of terrestrial infrastructure
- Navigation systems: Professional GPS with survey-grade accuracy and mapping capability
- Emergency beacons: Personal locator beacons and emergency satellite communication
- Cost: $2,000-8,000 for satellite communication equipment plus $100-500 monthly service costs

Mesh Network Infrastructure

- Community networks: High-power mesh networking providing community-wide internet and communication
- Wireless internet: Long-range wireless internet distribution and sharing systems
- Network management: Professional network management and security systems
- Redundant connections: Multiple internet connections with automatic failover capability
- Cost: $3,000-10,000 for community mesh network infrastructure and management

14.2 Sustainable Food Production Systems

Beyond food storage to a permanent food production capability that provides fresh, nutritious food while building soil health and creating increasingly productive agricultural systems.

Permaculture & Regenerative Agriculture
Integrated Food Production Systems

Permaculture systems create productive, sustainable food production that improves rather than degrades environmental conditions while providing increasing yields over time.

Fruit & Nut Tree Systems

- Orchard establishment: Diverse fruit and nut trees providing long-term food production
- Polyculture design: Multiple species integration maximizing production per square foot
- Soil improvement: Tree systems build soil health and carbon sequestration
- Water management: Tree systems providing natural water management and erosion control
- Cost: $3,000-10,000 for mature orchard establishment with irrigation and soil improvement

Vegetable Production Systems

- Raised bed systems: Intensive vegetable production with improved soil and drainage
- Season extension: Greenhouse, hoop house, and cold frame systems extend the growing season
- Companion planting: Integrated plant systems maximizing production and pest management
- Succession planting: Continuous harvest systems provide fresh food throughout the growing season
- Cost: $2,000-8,000 for intensive vegetable production systems with season extension

Integrated Pest Management

- Beneficial insects: Habitat creation and management for natural pest control
- Companion planting: Plant combinations providing natural pest deterrence
- Organic methods: Natural pest and disease management without chemical inputs
- Soil health: Healthy soil systems provide natural plant disease resistance
- Cost: $500-2,000 for integrated pest management systems and beneficial habitat

Livestock & Protein Production
Small-Scale Livestock Systems

Livestock systems provide meat, eggs, dairy, and other animal products while improving soil health through rotational grazing and integrated management.

Poultry Systems

- Layer flock management: 20-50 hens providing eggs for the family plus surplus for trade/sale
- Meat bird production: Seasonal meat bird production providing chicken, duck, or turkey
- Integrated systems: Poultry integration with vegetable production for pest control and fertilization
- Housing systems: Predator-proof housing with pasture rotation systems
- Cost: $2,000-6,000 for complete poultry production systems with housing and equipment

Small Ruminant Systems

- Goat production: Dairy goats provide milk, cheese, and meat production
- Sheep systems: Sheep provide wool, meat, and vegetation management

- Rotational grazing: Managed grazing improves pasture health and animal nutrition
- Processing capability: On-farm processing equipment for meat and dairy products
- Cost: $5,000-15,000 for small ruminant systems with housing, fencing, and equipment

Aquaculture Systems

- Fishpond systems: Catfish, tilapia, or trout production in pond or tank systems
- Aquaponics: Integrated fish and vegetable production in recirculating systems
- Water management: Pond systems providing water storage and fire protection
- Processing systems: On-farm fish processing and preservation equipment
- Cost: $3,000-12,000 for aquaculture systems with pumps, filtration, and processing

Food Processing & Preservation
Commercial-Scale Food Processing

Food processing systems enabling preservation of surplus production while creating value-added products for trade, sale, or long-term storage.

Preservation Systems

- Canning equipment: Commercial-grade pressure canners and water bath systems
- Dehydration systems: Large-capacity food dehydrators with solar and electric options
- Freezing systems: Large chest freezers with backup power and temperature monitoring
- Fermentation systems: Controlled fermentation for vegetables, dairy,

and meat preservation
- Cost: $3,000-8,000 for commercial-scale food preservation equipment

Value-Added Processing

- Dairy processing: Cheese making, butter production, and yogurt systems
- Meat processing: Grinding, sausage making, and curing equipment
- Grain processing: Flour milling, grain cleaning, and storage systems
- Beverage production: Cider, wine, beer, and other fermented beverage systems
- Cost: $2,000-10,000 for value-added food processing equipment and facilities

14.3 Economic Resilience & Alternative Systems

Building economic independence through alternative currencies, local trade networks, and sustainable business models that provide income and resource access independent of traditional economic systems.

Local Economy Development

Community Currency & Trade Systems

Alternative economic systems that keep wealth circulating within communities while providing recession-proof income and resource access.

Local Currency Systems

- Community currency: Local currency system encouraging community trade and resource circulation
- Time banking: A time-based currency system that exchanges services and skills
- Barter networks: Organized bartering systems with accounting and fairness management
- Skill exchanges: Professional skill sharing with credit systems and quality management

- Cost: $200-1,000 for community currency system development and administration

Local Business Development

- Service businesses: Emergency-related services, including preparedness consulting, training, and installation
- Product businesses: Value-added food production, craft goods, and preparedness equipment
- Repair services: Equipment repair, maintenance, and restoration services
- Education services: Skills training, workshops, and consulting services
- Cost: $2,000-15,000 for small business development, depending on business type and scale

Precious Metals & Alternative Assets
Wealth Preservation Systems

Alternative asset systems provide wealth preservation and transaction capability when traditional financial systems become unreliable or unavailable.

Precious Metals Investment

- Physical metals: Gold and silver coins and bars in secure storage
- Storage systems: Home safes, safety deposit boxes, and secure storage facilities
- Authentication systems: Testing equipment and procedures for precious metals verification
- Transaction systems: Knowledge and networks for precious metals transactions
- Cost: Market value of metals plus 5-10% premium and storage costs

Alternative Investments

- Land investment: Productive agricultural land providing both asset appreciation and income
- Equipment investment: High-quality equipment that retains value and provides income capability
- Commodity stockpiles: Strategic commodities that retain value and provide trade capability
- Skill development: Professional skills providing income capability independent of employment
- Cost: Varies significantly based on investment type and scale

Sustainable Business Models
Recession-Proof Income Streams

Business models that provide income during economic disruption while serving essential community needs and building long-term wealth.

Essential Service Businesses

- Water systems: Well drilling, pump installation, and water treatment services
- Power systems: Solar installation, generator service, and electrical system maintenance
- Food systems: Garden installation, livestock management, and food processing services
- Security systems: Security consulting, installation, and training services
- Cost: $5,000-25,000 for service business development with equipment and certification

Educational & Consulting Services

- Preparedness consulting: Family and business preparedness planning and implementation
- Skills training: Teaching preparedness skills, outdoor skills, and traditional crafts
- Community development: Facilitating community preparedness and

resilience projects
- Technical services: Specialized technical consulting in preparedness-related fields
- Cost: Professional development and certification costs $2,000-8,000

14.4 Psychological Resilience & Community Leadership

Building mental toughness, community leadership capability, and social systems that maintain morale, resolve conflicts, and organize effective collective action during extended challenges.

Mental Health & Psychological Preparation
Stress Inoculation & Mental Toughness
Psychological preparation systems that build mental resilience, stress tolerance, and decision-making capability under extreme pressure.

Stress Training Programs

- Cold exposure: Controlled cold exposure training builds stress tolerance and mental toughness
- Physical challenges: Structured physical challenges, building confidence and stress resilience
- Meditation practices: Regular meditation and mindfulness training for stress management
- Scenario training: Mental rehearsal of emergency scenarios, building confidence and decision-making
- Cost: $500-2,000 for stress training programs and mental conditioning

Family Mental Health Systems

- Counseling resources: Professional mental health support and family therapy resources
- Support networks: Community mental health support and peer counseling systems
- Stress management: Family stress management techniques and conflict

resolution skills
- Recreational systems: Entertainment, hobbies, and recreational activities, maintaining morale
- Cost: Mental health services $100-300 per session, plus recreational equipment and activities

Leadership Development & Community Organization
Community Leadership Systems

Leadership development builds the ability to organize community resources, resolve conflicts, and coordinate collective action during challenging times.

Leadership Training & Development

- Conflict resolution: Professional training in mediation, negotiation, and conflict resolution
- Group dynamics: Training in group leadership, meeting facilitation, and consensus building
- Emergency management: Training in incident command systems and emergency coordination
- Communication skills: Public speaking, persuasion, and community communication training
- Cost: $2,000-8,000 for comprehensive leadership development and training

Community Organization Systems

- Governance structures: Community decision-making systems and leadership structures
- Resource allocation: Fair and effective systems for community resource allocation
- Conflict resolution: Community conflict resolution and justice systems
- Collective action: Systems for organizing and coordinating community projects and responses

- Cost: Community development time investment plus organizational systems and training

Cultural & Social Systems
Community Culture Development
Social systems that maintain community cohesion, shared values, and mutual support during extended challenges while preserving knowledge and traditions.

Knowledge Preservation Systems

- Skill documentation: Systematic documentation of community skills and knowledge
- Library systems: Community libraries with practical knowledge and reference materials
- Teaching systems: Systematic knowledge transfer between generations and community members
- Cultural preservation: Maintaining cultural traditions, celebrations, and community identity
- Cost: $1,000-5,000 for knowledge preservation systems and cultural program development

Social Integration Programs

- Community events: Regular social events maintain community relationships and morale
- Mutual aid systems: Organized systems for community mutual assistance and support
- Youth development: Programs engaging youth in community preparedness and skill development
- Elder integration: Systems utilizing elder knowledge and experience in community development
- Cost: Community event and program costs $2,000-8,000 annually

CHAPTER 14

Long-Term Community Planning
Multi-Generational Resilience

Long-term planning systems that build community resilience across multiple generations while improving living standards and environmental conditions.

Succession Planning

- Knowledge transfer: Systematic transfer of critical knowledge and skills to the next generation
- Leadership development: Training and development of next-generation community leaders
- Asset management: Long-term management and preservation of community assets and resources
- Continuous improvement: Systems ensuring community resilience improve over multiple generations
- Cost: Long-term planning and development time investment plus educational resources

Community Infrastructure Development

- Physical infrastructure: Long-term development of community facilities, utilities, and transportation
- Social infrastructure: Development of community institutions, organizations, and social systems
- Economic infrastructure: Development of local economy, business systems, and financial institutions
- Educational infrastructure: Development of community education, training, and knowledge systems
- Cost: Major infrastructure investment $50,000-500,000+, depending on community size and projects

Chapter Summary: Building Advanced Long-Term Resilience

Advanced preparedness systems go beyond emergency survival to create sustainable, self-reliant communities that thrive during disruption while building stronger foundations for permanent security and prosperity. By implementing the advanced systems in this chapter, you'll have:

✓ **Energy independence** through comprehensive renewable systems and backup generation

✓ **Water independence** through well systems, rainwater harvesting, and water recycling

✓ **Food production capability** through permaculture, livestock, and food processing systems

✓ **Economic resilience** through local currencies, alternative investments, and sustainable businesses

✓ **Community leadership** through psychological preparation and organizational development

✓ **Long-term sustainability** through multi-generational planning and continuous improvement

Implementation Priority Order:

1. Basic renewable energy and water independence systems
2. Food production establishment and soil development
3. Economic diversification and alternative income development
4. Community organization and leadership development
5. Advanced infrastructure and long-term planning systems
6. Multi-generational sustainability and continuous improvement

Major Investment Categories:

- **Energy independence**: $40,000-90,000 for complete renewable energy systems
- **Water independence**: $30,000-80,000 for comprehensive water systems
- **Food production**: $15,000-50,000 for integrated food production systems
- **Economic systems**: $10,000-40,000 for business development and

alternative assets
- **Community development**: $5,000-25,000 for leadership and organizational systems
- **Total Investment**: $100,000-285,000 for comprehensive advanced resilience systems

Philosophical Shift: This chapter represents a fundamental shift from preparedness thinking to resilience living:

- **Preparedness mindset**: Temporary measures for emergency survival
- **Resilience mindset**: Permanent lifestyle improvements providing ongoing benefits
- **Sustainability focus**: Systems that improve rather than degrade over time
- **Community orientation**: Individual improvement contributing to collective strength

Long-Term Benefits: Advanced systems provide multiple benefits beyond emergency preparedness:

- **Reduced living costs**: Energy, water, and food independence, reducing monthly expenses
- **Improved health**: Fresh food, clean water, and reduced stress improve family health
- **Income generation**: Sustainable businesses and food production creating income streams
- **Environmental improvement**: Regenerative systems improving land and community health
- **Community strength**: Strong local relationships and mutual aid systems

Return on Investment: Advanced systems provide excellent long-term return on investment:

- **Energy systems**: 8-15% annual return through eliminated utility costs and net metering
- **Food systems**: 15-25% annual return through eliminated food costs and surplus sales
- **Water systems**: 5-10% annual return through eliminated water costs and improved reliability
- **Business systems**: Variable returns, but provide recession-proof income capability
- **Community systems**: Difficult to quantify, but provide substantial quality of life improvements

Integration with Previous Chapters: Advanced systems build on all previous preparedness investments:

- **Chapters 1-12**: Foundation systems becoming permanent infrastructure improvements
- **Chapter 13**: Technology systems enabling advanced monitoring and optimization
- **Chapter 14**: Advanced systems providing permanent lifestyle enhancement

The Complete Resilience Journey: The fourteen chapters represent a complete progression:

1. **Emergency preparedness** (Chapters 1-8): Surviving short-term disruptions
2. **Comprehensive preparedness** (Chapters 9-12): Thriving during extended challenges
3. **Advanced preparedness** (Chapter 13): Technology-enhanced optimization and efficiency
4. **Resilient living** (Chapter 14): Permanent lifestyle improvements and community development

Multi-Generational Perspective: Advanced systems provide benefits across multiple generations:

- **Immediate benefits**: Reduced living costs and improved emergency preparedness
- **Medium-term benefits**: Income generation and community development
- **Long-term benefits**: Asset appreciation and environmental improvement
- **Generational benefits**: Knowledge, skills, and assets transferred to children and grandchildren

Community Impact: Advanced preparedness creates positive community effects:

- **Economic development**: Local businesses and employment creation
- **Environmental improvement**: Regenerative agriculture and renewable energy adoption
- **Social strengthening**: Community organizations and mutual aid systems
- **Knowledge preservation**: Skills and traditions maintained for future generations

The Ultimate Goal: The ultimate goal of advanced preparedness is not just survival, but the creation of resilient communities that provide:

- **Security**: Multiple redundant systems ensuring family and community safety
- **Prosperity**: Sustainable systems providing ongoing economic benefits
- **Health**: Clean environment and nutritious food supporting optimal health
- **Community**: Strong relationships and mutual aid systems providing social support

- **Legacy**: Improved conditions and capabilities passed to future generations

This final chapter represents the pinnacle of preparedness thinking—the transition from emergency response to permanent lifestyle improvement that creates stronger, healthier, more prosperous, and more secure communities for current and future generations.

Appendix A

Local Resource Integration: Connecting with Community Emergency Services

"True preparedness extends beyond individual family supplies to include deep integration with local emergency services, community organizations, and regional resources that multiply your family's resilience through professional support and coordinated community response."

The most prepared families are those who understand, connect with, and actively participate in their local emergency management ecosystem. This integration transforms isolated family preparedness into coordinated community resilience while providing access to professional resources, early warning systems, and mutual aid networks that dramatically enhance your family's emergency capability.

Understanding Your Local Emergency Management Structure
Municipal Emergency Management
City/County Emergency Management Office

Every municipality has designated emergency management personnel responsible for coordinating disaster response, maintaining emergency plans, and providing public information during crises.

Key Services & Resources:

- **Emergency planning**: Community-wide emergency response plans and evacuation procedures

- **Early warning systems**: Official alerts, sirens, and notification systems for imminent threats
- **Resource coordination**: Emergency shelters, food distribution, medical care, and transportation
- **Public information**: Official information during emergencies, rumor control, and situation updates
- **Recovery assistance**: Disaster recovery resources, insurance liaison, and rebuilding coordination

How to Connect:

- **Office location**: Visit your city/county emergency management office in person
- **Contact information**: Obtain direct phone numbers, email addresses, and after-hours contacts
- **Alert registration**: Register for emergency alerts via text, email, and automated phone calls
- **Plan review**: Request copies of local emergency plans and evacuation routes
- **Meeting attendance**: Attend public meetings on emergency preparedness and community resilience

What to Learn:

- **Threat assessment**: Official assessment of natural and man-made hazards in your area
- **Evacuation zones**: Designated evacuation zones and routes for different threat scenarios
- **Shelter locations**: Official emergency shelters, capacity, and services provided
- **Communication procedures**: How officials will communicate with the public during emergencies
- **Resource allocation**: How emergency resources are distributed and

APPENDIX A

accessed during crises

Regional Emergency Coordination
State Emergency Management Agency

State-level emergency management provides resources, coordination, and expertise that exceed local capabilities during major disasters.

State-Level Resources:

- **National Guard**: Military resources for search and rescue, security, and logistics
- **State police**: Law enforcement coordination and highway management during evacuations
- **Health departments**: Medical resources, disease control, and public health coordination
- **Transportation departments**: Road maintenance, traffic management, and transportation resources
- **Environmental agencies**: Hazardous material response, water quality, and environmental monitoring

Federal Emergency Resources:

- **FEMA coordination**: Federal disaster declarations and resource allocation
- **Military assistance**: Department of Defense resources for major disaster response
- **Public health service**: CDC coordination for disease outbreaks and medical emergencies
- **Transportation security**: FAA, Coast Guard, and transportation security coordination
- **Communication systems**: National communication networks and emergency broadcasting

First Responder Services & Integration

Fire Department Services
Beyond Fire Suppression

Modern fire departments provide comprehensive emergency services extending far beyond fire suppression to include medical response, rescue operations, and hazardous material management.

Complete Fire Department Services:

- **Fire suppression**: Structure fires, wildland fires, vehicle fires, and industrial fires
- **Emergency medical**: Paramedic services, medical transport, and cardiac emergency response
- **Technical rescue**: Vehicle accidents, building collapse, confined space, and high-angle rescue
- **Hazardous materials**: Chemical spills, gas leaks, and environmental contamination response
- **Community education**: Fire prevention, CPR training, and emergency preparedness education

Building Relationships with Fire Services:

- **Station visits**: Visit local fire stations to meet personnel and learn about services
- **Training opportunities**: Attend CPR, first aid, and emergency response training offered by the fire department
- **Community programs**: Participate in fire safety inspections, smoke detector programs, and educational events
- **Volunteer opportunities**: Explore volunteer firefighter or auxiliary programs if available
- **Emergency planning**: Discuss your family emergency plans with local fire prevention officers

Fire Department Intelligence:

- **Response capabilities**: Types of equipment, personnel, and specialized capabilities available
- **Response times**: Average response times to your neighborhood and factors affecting response
- **Mutual aid agreements**: Neighboring departments providing backup resources
- **Communication procedures**: How to effectively communicate emergency information to dispatchers
- **Special programs**: Community emergency response training and neighborhood watch programs

Law Enforcement Integration
Police Services & Community Safety

Law enforcement provides security, traffic control, evacuation assistance, and emergency coordination that becomes critical during widespread emergencies.

Emergency Law Enforcement Services:

- **Security**: Crime prevention, looting prevention, and public order maintenance
- **Traffic management**: Evacuation route management, traffic control, and road closure coordination
- **Search and rescue**: Missing person searches, welfare checks, and emergency assistance
- **Communication**: Information relay, family notification, and emergency coordination
- **Special operations**: SWAT, bomb squad, and specialized emergency response teams

Law Enforcement Relationship Building:

- **Community policing**: Attend community policing meetings and neighborhood watch programs

- **Officer contact**: Meet the beat officers and community liaison officers for your area
- **Emergency procedures**: Learn police emergency procedures and communication protocols
- **Mutual aid**: Understand mutual aid agreements with neighboring jurisdictions
- **Special programs**: Participate in citizen police academies and emergency volunteer programs

What Police Want You to Know:

- **Emergency communication**: Proper procedures for emergency calls and information reporting
- **Evacuation cooperation**: How to comply with evacuation orders and traffic management
- **Security awareness**: Crime prevention during emergencies and suspicious activity reporting
- **Family identification**: Emergency identification procedures and family accountability systems
- **Resource limitations**: Understanding police capabilities and limitations during major emergencies

Emergency Medical Services
EMS & Hospital System Integration

Emergency medical services provide life-saving medical care, patient transport, and coordination with hospital systems during medical emergencies and disasters.

Comprehensive EMS Services:

- **Emergency response**: Paramedic and EMT response to medical emergencies
- **Patient transport**: Ambulance transport to appropriate medical facilities

APPENDIX A

- **Mass casualty**: Multiple patient incidents and disaster medical response
- **Special operations**: Urban search and rescue medical support, hazmat medical response
- **Community health**: Public health support, vaccination clinics, and health screening

Building EMS Relationships:

- **Training opportunities**: CPR, first aid, and emergency medical training from EMS providers
- **Hospital tours**: Visit local emergency departments and trauma centers
- **Medical planning**: Discuss family medical needs with EMS community outreach personnel
- **Volunteer programs**: Explore volunteer EMS opportunities or auxiliary support roles
- **Education programs**: Attend community health and safety education programs

Critical EMS Information:

- **Hospital locations**: Nearest emergency departments, trauma centers, and specialty hospitals
- **Response protocols**: How EMS triages and prioritizes emergency calls
- **Medical identification**: Medical alert systems and emergency medical information
- **Insurance coordination**: How EMS coordinates with insurance and patient information
- **Disaster medical**: Hospital surge capacity and alternate care facilities during disasters

Community Organization Networks

Religious & Community Organizations
Faith-Based Emergency Support

Religious organizations often provide the most immediate and sustained emergency assistance through established networks, facilities, and volunteer systems.

Church & Religious Organization Resources:

- **Shelter facilities**: Large meeting halls, kitchens, and sleeping accommodations
- **Food programs**: Food banks, community kitchens, and meal distribution systems
- **Volunteer networks**: Organized volunteer systems with leadership and coordination
- **Communication systems**: Established communication networks reaching community members
- **Recovery assistance**: Long-term recovery support, counseling, and rebuilding assistance

Community Center Resources:

- **Meeting facilities**: Large spaces for community meetings and emergency coordination
- **Equipment resources**: Sound systems, tables, chairs, and event coordination equipment
- **Programming expertise**: Event planning, coordination, and community mobilization experience
- **Local knowledge**: Deep understanding of community needs, resources, and relationships
- **Ongoing programs**: Existing programs that can be adapted for emergency response

Building Community Organization Relationships:

- **Regular attendance**: Participate in religious services, community events, and volunteer activities
- **Leadership contact**: Meet with religious leaders, community center directors, and program coordinators
- **Volunteer participation**: Volunteer for community service projects and emergency preparedness activities
- **Skill sharing**: Offer your preparedness knowledge and skills to community organizations
- **Resource coordination**: Discuss how your family preparedness can support community emergency response

Neighborhood Organizations
Homeowner Associations & Neighborhood Groups

Neighborhood organizations provide the most immediate community support and coordinate response during emergencies affecting your specific area.

Neighborhood Organization Capabilities:

- **Communication networks**: Established communication systems reaching all neighborhood residents
- **Resource coordination**: Neighborhood resource sharing and mutual aid coordination
- **Local knowledge**: Detailed knowledge of neighborhood infrastructure, resources, and vulnerabilities
- **Meeting facilities**: Regular meeting locations and established leadership structures
- **Maintenance resources**: Landscaping equipment, tools, and facility maintenance capabilities

Starting or Strengthening Neighborhood Preparedness:

- **Emergency planning**: Organize neighborhood emergency planning meetings and resource sharing

- **Communication systems**: Establish neighborhood communication networks using social media, email, and radio
- **Skill inventory**: Catalog neighborhood skills, resources, and emergency capabilities
- **Mutual aid agreements**: Develop formal or informal mutual aid agreements with neighbors
- **Regular training**: Organize neighborhood training in CPR, first aid, and emergency response

Service Clubs & Civic Organizations

Rotary, Lions, Kiwanis, & Similar Organizations. Service clubs bring together community leaders, professionals, and volunteers with resources, connections, and coordination experience that is valuable during emergencies.

Service Club Emergency Capabilities:

- **Professional networks**: Members with professional skills in medical, legal, construction, and business fields
- **Financial resources**: Access to emergency funding, grants, and fundraising capabilities
- **Volunteer coordination**: Experienced in volunteer management and project coordination
- **Regional connections**: Connections with similar organizations in surrounding communities
- **Equipment access**: Access to professional equipment through member businesses

Connecting with Service Organizations:

- **Meeting attendance**: Attend meetings as a guest to learn about the organization and membership
- **Volunteer participation**: Volunteer for service projects and community emergency preparedness initiatives

- **Professional contribution**: Offer your professional skills to the organization's emergency preparedness efforts
- **Membership consideration**: Consider joining organizations aligned with your values and interests
- **Partnership development**: Develop partnerships between service clubs and neighborhood preparedness groups

Utility & Infrastructure Services
Electric & Gas Utilities
Power & Gas Emergency Coordination

Utility companies provide critical infrastructure services and have sophisticated emergency response capabilities that can support community emergency response.

Utility Emergency Services:

- **Outage restoration**: Priority restoration procedures and estimated restoration times
- **Emergency shutoffs**: Gas and electric service emergency shutoff procedures and coordination
- **Infrastructure protection**: Critical infrastructure protection and backup power systems
- **Communication systems**: Customer communication during outages and emergency situations
- **Mobile services**: Emergency mobile power and gas service restoration capabilities

Building Utility Relationships:

- **Emergency contacts**: Obtain emergency contact numbers for utility companies serving your area
- **Outage reporting**: Learn proper procedures for reporting outages and emergency situations
- **Priority service**: Investigate priority service programs for medical

equipment and special needs
- **Restoration procedures**: Understand utility restoration priorities and estimated timeframes
- **Safety education**: Attend utility-sponsored safety education programs and emergency preparedness

Utility Coordination Information:

- **Service territories**: Which utilities serve your area and backup/mutual aid agreements
- **Infrastructure vulnerabilities**: Known infrastructure vulnerabilities and improvement plans
- **Emergency procedures**: Utility emergency response procedures and coordination with emergency management
- **Customer programs**: Special programs for medical needs, elderly customers, and emergency assistance
- **Communication methods**: How utilities communicate with customers during emergencies

Water & Sewer Services
Water System Emergency Management

Water and sewer utilities manage critical life-safety infrastructure with sophisticated emergency response and public health coordination.

Water Utility Emergency Capabilities:

- **Water quality monitoring**: Continuous water quality monitoring and contamination response
- **Infrastructure protection**: Water system security and critical infrastructure protection
- **Emergency supply**: Emergency water distribution and alternative supply coordination
- **Public health coordination**: Coordination with public health agencies for water safety

- **Communication systems**: Public notification systems for water emergencies and advisories

Sewer System Emergency Services:

- **System monitoring**: Sewer system monitoring and overflow prevention
- **Emergency repairs**: Rapid response to sewer system failures and blockages
- **Public health protection**: Coordination with health agencies to prevent disease transmission
- **Environmental protection**: Environmental monitoring and contamination prevention
- **Customer communication**: Public notification of sewer system emergencies and advisories

Telecommunications Services
Communication Infrastructure Emergency Support

Telecommunications providers maintain a communication infrastructure critical for emergency response and public safety coordination.

Telecom Emergency Services:

- **Priority service**: Emergency services priority for first responders and critical facilities
- **Mobile resources**: Cell towers on wheels (COWs) and mobile communication equipment
- **Infrastructure protection**: Communication infrastructure hardening and backup power systems
- **Emergency broadcasting**: Coordination with emergency broadcasting and alert systems
- **Public communication**: Public Wi-Fi and communication services during emergencies

Healthcare System Integration

Hospital & Medical Systems

Healthcare Emergency Preparedness

Hospitals and healthcare systems maintain sophisticated emergency preparedness capabilities, including surge capacity, specialized treatment, and coordination with public health agencies.

Hospital Emergency Capabilities:

- **Emergency departments**: 24/7 emergency medical care and trauma treatment
- **Surge capacity**: Ability to expand capacity during mass casualty incidents
- **Specialized services**: Trauma centers, cardiac care, pediatric emergency care, and psychiatric services
- **Medical coordination**: Coordination with EMS, public health, and other hospitals
- **Disaster medical**: Disaster medical response teams and mobile medical capabilities

Public Health Services:

- **Disease surveillance**: Monitoring and response to disease outbreaks and public health threats
- **Emergency medical**: Mass vaccination clinics, medical countermeasures, and public health response
- **Environmental health**: Food safety, water quality, and environmental health monitoring
- **Health communication**: Public health information and emergency health advisories
- **Vulnerable populations**: Special programs for elderly, disabled, and medically vulnerable residents

Healthcare Relationship Building:

- **Hospital tours**: Visit local hospital emergency departments and learn about services
- **Physician relationships**: Establish relationships with local physicians and medical practices
- **Public health contact**: Contact the local public health department and learn about services
- **Medical training**: Attend medical training offered by hospitals and public health agencies
- **Special needs planning**: Discuss special medical needs with healthcare providers

Veterinary Services

Animal Emergency Care & Support Veterinary services provide emergency care for animals and coordinate with emergency management for animal rescue and care during disasters.

Veterinary Emergency Services:

- **Emergency animal care**: 24-hour emergency veterinary services and trauma treatment
- **Animal rescue**: Animal search and rescue during disasters and emergency situations
- **Public health**: Coordination with public health agencies for animal disease control
- **Animal sheltering**: Emergency animal sheltering and care during evacuations
- **Livestock services**: Large animal emergency care and livestock emergency management

Educational Institution Resources
School District Emergency Systems
School Emergency Preparedness

School districts maintain comprehensive emergency preparedness systems, including early dismissal procedures, emergency communication, and

coordination with parents and emergency services.
School Emergency Capabilities:

- **Student accountability**: Student tracking and parent notification systems during emergencies
- **Emergency communication**: School-to-parent communication systems and emergency information
- **Facility resources**: School facilities as emergency shelters and community resource centers
- **Transportation**: School bus transportation for evacuations and emergency transport
- **Emergency supplies**: School emergency supplies, food service, and medical capabilities

University & College Resources:

- **Emergency management**: University emergency management offices and campus security services
- **Medical services**: Campus medical centers and student health services
- **Research capabilities**: University research capabilities in emergency management and public health
- **Communication systems**: Campus communication systems and emergency notification
- **Community resources**: University facilities and resources available to the surrounding community

Business & Economic Networks
Chamber of Commerce & Business Networks
Business Community Emergency Support Local businesses and chambers of commerce provide essential services, employment, and economic stability during emergency recovery periods.
Business Emergency Capabilities:

APPENDIX A

- **Essential services**: Grocery stores, pharmacies, gas stations, and other essential business services
- **Employment**: Economic stability through continued employment during emergency recovery
- **Supply chains**: Business supply chain management and resource coordination
- **Professional services**: Legal, financial, medical, and technical professional services
- **Equipment resources**: Business equipment, facilities, and specialized capabilities

Building Business Relationships:

- **Chamber membership**: Join the local chamber of commerce and business networking organizations
- **Professional networking**: Build relationships with local business leaders and service providers
- **Emergency planning**: Participate in business emergency planning and continuity initiatives
- **Mutual aid**: Develop mutual aid relationships with local businesses and service providers
- **Skill exchange**: Offer your skills to local businesses in exchange for services and resources

Financial Institution Coordination
Banking & Financial Emergency Services

Banks and credit unions maintain emergency procedures for financial services access during emergencies and coordinate with emergency management for community support.

Financial Emergency Services:

- **Emergency access**: Emergency procedures for account access during system outages

- **Cash availability**: ATM management and cash distribution during emergencies
- **Loan assistance**: Emergency loan programs and disaster recovery financing
- **Insurance coordination**: Coordination with insurance companies for claim processing
- **Business continuity**: Financial institution business continuity planning and services

Technology & Communication Networks
Amateur Radio Networks
Ham Radio Emergency Communication

Amateur radio operators provide critical emergency communication services and maintain sophisticated communication networks that support emergency services and public safety.

Amateur Radio Emergency Capabilities:

- **Emergency communication**: Long-distance communication when normal systems fail
- **Health and welfare**: Personal message handling for families during emergencies
- **Emergency coordination**: Communication support for emergency management and first responders
- **Public service**: Weather spotting, emergency information relay, and public safety support
- **Technical expertise**: Electronic and communication technical support during emergencies

Connecting with Amateur Radio:

- **Local clubs**: Contact local amateur radio clubs and attend meetings
- **Licensing**: Obtain an amateur radio license through training and testing programs

- **Emergency training**: Participate in emergency communication training and drills
- **Equipment**: Learn about amateur radio equipment and emergency communication capabilities
- **Volunteer service**: Volunteer for amateur radio emergency service organizations

Internet Service Providers
Digital Communication Emergency Support

Internet service providers maintain critical communication infrastructure and provide emergency communication services during disasters.

ISP Emergency Services:

- **Infrastructure hardening**: Internet infrastructure protection and backup power systems
- **Emergency access**: Public Wi-Fi and emergency internet access during outages
- **Priority service**: Priority internet service for emergency services and critical facilities
- **Communication coordination**: Coordination with emergency management for communication support
- **Public information**: Emergency information distribution and public communication support

Creating Your Local Resource Integration Plan
Systematic Community Connection
Phased Approach to Community Integration

Building comprehensive community connections requires a systematic approach focusing on the most critical relationships first while gradually expanding your network.

Phase 1: Emergency Services (Month 1-2)

- Contact the local emergency management office and obtain emergency

plans
- Visit the local fire station and meet the fire department personnel
- Attend a police community meeting and meet local law enforcement
- Register for emergency alerts and notification systems
- Obtain emergency contact information for all services

Phase 2: Healthcare & Utilities (Month 3-4)

- Tour the local hospital emergency department and meet key personnel
- Contact utility companies and learn emergency procedures
- Establish relationships with local physicians and healthcare providers
- Connect with the public health department and learn about services
- Investigate priority service programs for special needs

Phase 3: Community Organizations (Month 5-6)

- Attend religious services or community organization meetings
- Join or contact neighborhood organizations and homeowner associations
- Connect with service clubs and civic organizations
- Participate in community volunteer activities and emergency preparedness
- Build relationships with neighbors and community leaders

Phase 4: Specialized Networks (Ongoing)

- Connect with amateur radio clubs and consider licensing
- Build relationships with local businesses and professional services
- Participate in school emergency planning and communication
- Develop mutual aid relationships and resource-sharing agreements
- Continue expanding community connections and relationships

Documentation & Communication Systems

APPENDIX A

Community Resource Database: Maintain a comprehensive database of community resources, contacts, and capabilities for easy access during emergencies.

Essential Information to Collect:

- **Contact information**: Names, phone numbers, addresses, and email addresses
- **Service capabilities**: What services each organization provides during emergencies
- **Resource availability**: What resources each contact can provide or access
- **Communication methods**: How to reach each contact during emergencies
- **Mutual aid agreements**: What each contact expects in exchange for assistance

Communication Integration:

- **Multiple contact methods**: Phone, email, radio, and in-person contact information
- **Emergency procedures**: How each organization operates during different emergency scenarios
- **Coordination systems**: How different organizations coordinate with each other
- **Information sharing**: How to share information with community contacts during emergencies
- **Regular updates**: System for maintaining current contact information and capabilities

Chapter Summary: Building Comprehensive Community Integration

Local resource integration transforms individual family preparedness into coordinated community resilience by connecting with professional emergency services, community organizations, and regional support networks. By implementing comprehensive community integration, you'll have:

✓ **Professional emergency support** through relationships with fire, police, and emergency management

✓ **Healthcare system access** via connections with hospitals, physicians, and public health agencies

✓ **Community organization resources** through religious groups, service clubs, and neighborhood networks

✓ **Infrastructure coordination** with utilities, telecommunications, and transportation services

✓ **Regional support networks** connecting your family to broader emergency management systems

✓ **Mutual aid relationships** providing both support to and assistance from community members

Implementation Benefits:

- **Enhanced emergency response**: Professional emergency services are aware of your family's needs and capabilities
- **Early warning access**: Official emergency alerts and information from multiple sources
- **Resource multiplication**: Access to community resources beyond individual family capability
- **Recovery acceleration**: Community connections accelerating post-emergency recovery and rebuilding
- **Social resilience**: Strong community relationships providing emotional and practical support

Key Success Factors:

- **Reciprocal relationships**: Offer your skills and resources to community organizations
- **Regular participation**: Maintain ongoing relationships through

regular contact and participation
- **Clear communication**: Ensure community contacts understand your family's capabilities and needs
- **Documentation systems**: Maintain current information about community contacts and resources
- **Continuous expansion**: Gradually expand community connections and deepen existing relationships

Long-Term Community Benefits: Community integration creates positive feedback loops that strengthen both individual family preparedness and overall community resilience:

- **Information sharing**: Community members share preparedness knowledge and best practices
- **Resource efficiency**: Coordinated resource sharing reduces individual preparation costs
- **Collective capability**: Community coordination enables projects beyond individual family capability
- **Cultural change**: Community preparedness is becoming normal and expected rather than unusual
- **Resilience multiplication**: Strong communities making individual families more secure and capable

The Ultimate Goal: The goal of local resource integration is to create resilient communities where:

- **No family stands alone** during emergencies
- **Professional resources** are effectively coordinated with community self-help
- **Information flows quickly** through multiple trusted communication channels
- **Resources are shared efficiently** based on need and capability
- **Recovery happens faster** through coordinated community effort

Local resource integration represents the difference between isolated family preparedness and true community resilience. While individual preparation provides security, community integration provides multiplication of that security through professional support, shared resources, and coordinated response that makes every family safer and more capable.

Appendix B

Supplier & Product Recommendations: High, Mid, and Budget Options

"Quality preparedness equipment doesn't always require premium pricing—strategic product selection provides reliable capability at every budget level while avoiding false economy on critical life-safety items."

This comprehensive guide provides specific product recommendations across all preparedness categories, with high-end, mid-range, and budget options that deliver reliable performance. Each recommendation includes supplier information, key features, and value analysis to help you make informed purchasing decisions that match your budget and requirements.

Water Storage & Purification Systems
Water Storage Containers
Premium Choice: Aquatainer Water Storage System

- **Product**: Reliance Aquatainer 7-Gallon Water Container with Spigot
- **Supplier**: Amazon, REI, Walmart
- **Price**: $25-35 per container
- **Features**: BPA-free construction, built-in spigot, stackable design, 5-year warranty
- **Why Premium**: Exceptional durability, convenient dispensing, long warranty period

Mid-Range Choice: Water Brick Stackable Containers

- **Product**: WaterBrick 3.5-Gallon Stackable Water Storage
- **Supplier**: Emergency Essentials, Amazon, Home Depot
- **Price**: $35-45 per container
- **Features**: Modular stacking system, dual handles, spill-proof cap
- **Why Mid-Range**: Space-efficient storage, good durability, reasonable cost per gallon

Budget Choice: Generic Water Storage Barrels

- **Product**: 55-Gallon Food-Grade Water Barrel
- **Supplier**: Emergency Preparedness suppliers, Craigslist, local distributors
- **Price**: $45-75 per barrel
- **Features**: Large capacity, food-grade plastic, basic functionality
- **Why Budget**: Lowest cost per gallon, simple and reliable, minimal features

Water Purification Systems
Premium Choice: Berkey Gravity-Fed System

- **Product**: Big Berkey Stainless Steel Water Filter
- **Supplier**: Berkeley Water Filters (direct), Amazon
- **Price**: $350-450 complete system
- **Features**: Removes bacteria, viruses, chemicals, and has a 6,000-gallon filter life
- **Why Premium**: Superior filtration capability, long filter life, no electricity required

Mid-Range Choice: Katadyn Pocket Filter

- **Product**: Katadyn Pocket Water Microfilter

- **Supplier**: REI, Amazon, camping supply stores
- **Price**: $180-220 per filter
- **Features**: 13,000-gallon cartridge life, silver-impregnated ceramic
- **Why Mid-Range**: Excellent reliability, long cartridge life, compact design

Budget Choice: LifeStraw Personal Filters

- **Product**: LifeStraw Personal Water Filter (4-pack)
- **Supplier**: Amazon, Target, Walmart
- **Price**: $60-80 for 4-pack
- **Features**: 1,000-gallon capacity each, no batteries, lightweight
- **Why Budget**: Very affordable, proven effectiveness, individual use capability

Food Storage & Preparation Systems
Long-Term Food Storage
Premium Choice: Mountain House Freeze-Dried Meals

- **Product**: Mountain House Essential Assortment Bucket
- **Supplier**: Mountain House (direct), REI, Emergency Essentials
- **Price**: $180-220 per bucket (28 servings)
- **Features**: 30-year shelf life, excellent taste, just add water preparation
- **Why Premium**: Superior taste and nutrition, longest shelf life, trusted brand

Mid-Range Choice: Augason Farms Emergency Food

- **Product**: Augason Farms 30-Day Emergency Food Supply
- **Supplier**: Walmart, Amazon, Costco
- **Price**: $130-180 per 30-day supply
- **Features**: 25-year shelf life, balanced nutrition, variety of meals
- **Why Mid-Range**: Good value per meal, decent taste, widely available

Budget Choice: Bulk Rice and Beans

- **Product**: White Rice (25 lbs) + Pinto Beans (25 lbs) + Storage Buckets
- **Supplier**: Costco, Sam's Club, LDS Preparedness Manual suppliers
- **Price**: $45-75 for 50 lbs total
- **Features**: Complete protein combination, 20+ year storage life, versatile
- **Why Budget**: Lowest cost per calorie, maximum storage life, proven nutrition

Cooking Equipment
Premium Choice: Jetboil Genesis Basecamp System

- **Product**: Jetboil Genesis Basecamp Cooking System
- **Supplier**: REI, Amazon, outdoor retailers
- **Price**: $200-250 per system
- **Features**: Two-burner system, wind-resistant, efficient fuel use
- **Why Premium**: Fast cooking, fuel efficient, reliable ignition, weather resistant

Mid-Range Choice: Coleman Dual-Fuel Stove

- **Product**: Coleman Dual Fuel 2-Burner Stove
- **Supplier**: Amazon, Walmart, sporting goods stores
- **Price**: $80-120 per stove
- **Features**: Burns gas or liquid fuel, two adjustable burners, wind guards
- **Why Mid-Range**: Fuel flexibility, proven reliability, good heat control

Budget Choice: Emergency Fuel Tablets

- **Product**: Esbit Solid Fuel Tablets with Folding Stove
- **Supplier**: Amazon, military surplus stores
- **Price**: $15-25 for the stove and 100 tablets

APPENDIX B

- **Features**: Compact storage, no liquid fuel, windproof burning
- **Why Budget**: Extremely affordable, compact, and no moving parts to break

Medical & First Aid Supplies
First Aid Kits
Premium Choice: Adventure Medical Kits Professional

- **Product**: Adventure Medical Mountain Series Mountaineer Kit
- **Supplier**: REI, Amazon, Adventure Medical Kits (direct)
- **Price**: $160-200 per kit
- **Features**: Comprehensive supplies, medical-grade components, detailed instructions
- **Why Premium**: Professional-quality supplies, extensive contents, excellent organization

Mid-Range Choice: First Aid Only Large Kit

- **Product**: First Aid Only 299-Piece All-Purpose Kit
- **Supplier**: Amazon, Walmart, office supply stores
- **Price**: $60-90 per kit
- **Features**: 299 pieces, hard case, basic medication included
- **Why Mid-Range**: Good quantity of supplies, organized storage, reasonable quality

Budget Choice: DIY First Aid Kit

- **Product**: Build your own using generic supplies
- **Supplier**: Dollar store, pharmacy, generic medical suppliers
- **Price**: $25-40 for equivalent supplies
- **Features**: Customizable contents, generic but functional supplies
- **Why Budget**: Lowest cost, tailored to family needs, upgradeable over time

Prescription Medication Management
Premium Choice: PillPack Pro Medication Organizer

- **Product**: PillPack Pro Weekly Organizer with Locking Lid
- **Supplier**: Amazon, pharmacy chains, medical supply companies
- **Price**: $35-50 per organizer
- **Features**: Secure locking, large compartments, clear labeling
- **Why Premium**: Secure storage, excellent organization, durable construction

Mid-Range Choice: Pill Organizer with Alarms

- **Product**: MedCenter Monthly Pill Organizer with Talking Alarm
- **Supplier**: Amazon, CVS, Walgreens
- **Price**: $20-35 per organizer
- **Features**: Audio reminders, monthly organization, clear compartments
- **Why Mid-Range**: Reminder functionality, good capacity, reasonable price

Budget Choice: Weekly Pill Organizers

- **Product**: 7-Day Pill Organizer (4-pack)
- **Supplier**: Dollar stores, Walmart, Amazon basics
- **Price**: $8-15 for 4-pack
- **Features**: Basic 7-day organization, clear compartments, compact size
- **Why Budget**: Very affordable, simple functionality, widely available

Tools & Repair Equipment
Multi-Tools & Knives
Premium Choice: Leatherman Wave Plus

- **Product**: Leatherman Wave Plus Multi-Tool
- **Supplier**: Leatherman (direct), REI, Amazon

- **Price**: $120-150 per tool
- **Features**: 18 tools, replaceable wire cutters, 25-year warranty
- **Why Premium**: Superior build quality, extensive warranty, replaceable components

Mid-Range Choice: Gerber MP600 Multi-Tool

- **Product**: Gerber MP600 Needlenose Multi-Tool
- **Supplier**: Amazon, Home Depot, sporting goods stores
- **Price**: $60-90 per tool
- **Features**: One-hand opening, locking blades, belt holster included
- **Why Mid-Range**: Good quality, one-hand operation, competitive pricing

Budget Choice: Generic Multi-Tool Set

- **Product**: 15-in-1 Multi-Tool with Sheath
- **Supplier**: Harbor Freight, Amazon, discount tool stores
- **Price**: $15-25 per tool
- **Features**: Basic tools, folding design, and included sheath
- **Why Budget**: Very affordable, covers basic needs, widely available

Hand Tools
Premium Choice: Klein Tools Electrician Set

- **Product**: Klein Tools 32-Piece Homeowner Tool Set
- **Supplier**: Home Depot, Amazon, electrical supply stores
- **Price**: $150-200 per set
- **Features**: Professional-grade tools, lifetime warranty, organized case
- **Why Premium**: Professional quality, comprehensive set, excellent warranty

Mid-Range Choice: Craftsman Tool Set

- **Product**: Craftsman 230-Piece Mechanics Tool Set
- **Supplier**: Lowe's, Amazon, Sears
- **Price**: $120-180 per set
- **Features**: 230 pieces, organized case, limited lifetime warranty
- **Why Mid-Range**: Good tool variety, organized storage, brand reputation

Budget Choice: Harbor Freight Tool Kit

- **Product**: Pittsburgh 130-Piece Tool Kit
- **Supplier**: Harbor Freight Tools
- **Price**: $40-70 per set
- **Features**: Basic hand tools, blow-molded case, adequate quality
- **Why Budget**: Very affordable, covers basic needs, and local availability

Power & Communication Systems
Portable Power Stations
Premium Choice: Goal Zero Yeti 1500X

- **Product**: Goal Zero Yeti 1500X Portable Power Station
- **Supplier**: Goal Zero (direct), REI, Amazon
- **Price**: $1,800-2,200 per unit
- **Features**: 1,516 Wh capacity, multiple output types, expandable with solar
- **Why Premium**: Huge capacity, excellent build quality, comprehensive warranty

Mid-Range Choice: Jackery Explorer 1000

- **Product**: Jackery Explorer 1000 Portable Power Station
- **Supplier**: Amazon, Costco, solar supply companies
- **Price**: $900-1,200 per unit
- **Features**: 1,002 Wh capacity, pure sine wave, LCD display

- **Why Mid-Range**: Good capacity-to-price ratio, reliable brand, user-friendly

Budget Choice: Power Bank Collection

- **Product**: Anker PowerCore 26800 (4-pack)
- **Supplier**: Amazon, Best Buy, electronics stores
- **Price**: $200-300 for 4-pack
- **Features**: 26,800 mAh each, multiple USB ports, compact size
- **Why Budget**: Very affordable per unit, portable, proven reliability

Two-Way Radios
Premium Choice: Motorola MOTOTRBO

- **Product**: Motorola XPR 7550 Digital Radio
- **Supplier**: Motorola dealers, Amazon, communications companies
- **Price**: $400-600 per radio
- **Features**: Digital technology, encryption capable, rugged construction
- **Why Premium**: Professional grade, excellent range, advanced features

Mid-Range Choice: Midland GXT Series

- **Product**: Midland GXT1000VP4 2-Way Radio (4-pack)
- **Supplier**: Amazon, Walmart, electronics stores
- **Price**: $150-220 for 4-pack
- **Features**: 50-channel GMRS, weather alerts, rechargeable batteries
- **Why Mid-Range**: Good range, weather features, reasonable price per unit

Budget Choice: Baofeng UV-5R

- **Product**: Baofeng UV-5R Dual Band Radio (4-pack)
- **Supplier**: Amazon, amateur radio dealers

- **Price**: $80-120 for 4-pack
- **Features**: VHF/UHF dual band, programmable, external antenna capable
- **Why Budget**: Very affordable, amateur radio capable, extensive features

Shelter & Warmth Systems
Emergency Shelters
Premium Choice: Big Agnes Copper Spur

- **Product**: Big Agnes Copper Spur HV UL4 Tent
- **Supplier**: REI, Amazon, outdoor retailers
- **Price**: $600-750 per tent
- **Features**: Ultralight, spacious interior, excellent weather protection
- **Why Premium**: Superior materials, innovative design, minimal weight

Mid-Range Choice: Coleman Instant Cabin

- **Product**: Coleman Instant Cabin Tent (6-person)
- **Supplier**: Amazon, Walmart, sporting goods stores
- **Price**: $200-300 per tent
- **Features**: 1-minute setup, spacious interior, weather-resistant
- **Why Mid-Range**: Quick setup, good space, family-friendly features

Budget Choice: Generic Dome Tent

- **Product**: 4-Person Dome Tent with Rainfly
- **Supplier**: Walmart, Amazon, discount outdoor stores
- **Price**: $50-90 per tent
- **Features**: Basic dome design, included rainfly, compact storage
- **Why Budget**: Very affordable, covers basic shelter needs, widely available

Sleeping Systems

Premium Choice: Western Mountaineering Sleeping Bags

- **Product**: Western Mountaineering UltraLite Sleeping Bag
- **Supplier**: REI, outdoor specialty stores
- **Price**: $400-600 per bag
- **Features**: 850-fill down, -10°F rating, lifetime warranty
- **Why Premium**: Superior insulation, excellent temperature rating, long warranty

Mid-Range Choice: REI Co-op Trail Pod

- **Product**: REI Co-op Trail Pod 29 Sleeping Bag
- **Supplier**: REI stores and website
- **Price**: $150-220 per bag
- **Features**: Synthetic insulation, 29°F rating, machine washable
- **Why Mid-Range**: Good warmth-to-weight ratio, easy care, member dividends

Budget Choice: Coleman Brazos Sleeping Bags

- **Product**: Coleman Brazos Cold Weather Sleeping Bag (4-pack)
- **Supplier**: Walmart, Amazon, sporting goods stores
- **Price**: $120-180 for 4-pack
- **Features**: 20°F rating, polyester fill, stuff sack included
- **Why Budget**: Very affordable per bag, adequate warmth, family sizing

Security & Self-Defense Equipment

Personal Protection Tools

Premium Choice: SABRE Pepper Spray

- **Product**: SABRE Advanced 3-in-1 Pepper Spray (4-pack)
- **Supplier**: Amazon, police supply stores, SABRE direct

- **Price**: $60-90 for 4-pack
- **Features**: 3-in-1 formula, 35 bursts, practice spray included
- **Why Premium**: Law enforcement grade, maximum effectiveness, training included

Mid-Range Choice: Mace Brand Defense Spray

- **Product**: Mace Brand Triple Action Personal Defense Spray
- **Supplier**: Amazon, sporting goods stores, pharmacies
- **Price**: $35-50 for 4-pack
- **Features**: Triple action formula, flip-top safety, belt holster
- **Why Mid-Range**: Trusted brand, good features, reasonable price

Budget Choice: Generic Pepper Spray

- **Product**: Personal Defense Pepper Spray (4-pack)
- **Supplier**: Walmart, Amazon, discount stores
- **Price**: $15-25 for 4-pack
- **Features**: Basic pepper spray, keychain attachment, safety cap
- **Why Budget**: Very affordable, meets basic protection needs, widely available

Home Security Systems
Premium Choice: Ring Alarm Pro Security System

- **Product**: Ring Alarm 14-Piece Kit with Professional Monitoring
- **Supplier**: Amazon, Best Buy, Ring Direct
- **Price**: $300-450 plus monitoring fees
- **Features**: Professional monitoring, smartphone control, expandable system
- **Why Premium**: Professional monitoring, comprehensive features, brand reputation

APPENDIX B

Mid-Range Choice: SimpliSafe Security System

- **Product**: SimpliSafe 12-Piece Wireless Security System
- **Supplier**: SimpliSafe direct, Amazon, Best Buy
- **Price**: $200-350 plus monitoring
- **Features**: Wireless installation, cellular monitoring, battery backup
- **Why Mid-Range**: Easy installation, reliable monitoring, competitive pricing

Budget Choice: DIY Door/Window Alarms

- **Product**: GE Personal Security Window/Door Alarm (10-pack)
- **Supplier**: Amazon, Home Depot, Lowe's
- **Price**: $40-70 for 10-pack
- **Features**: 120dB alarm, magnetic switch, easy installation
- **Why Budget**: Very affordable, simple operation, no monthly fees

Transportation & Vehicle Equipment
Vehicle Emergency Kits
Premium Choice: AAA Severe Weather Road Kit

- **Product**: AAA Severe Weather Emergency Road Kit
- **Supplier**: AAA stores, Amazon, automotive stores
- **Price**: $150-220 per kit
- **Features**: 76 pieces, premium jumper cables, road flares, tools
- **Why Premium**: Comprehensive contents, quality components, AAA backing

Mid-Range Choice: Lifeline Emergency Kit

- **Product**: Lifeline 4388AAA 42-Piece Emergency Kit
- **Supplier**: Amazon, Walmart, auto parts stores
- **Price**: $60-90 per kit

- **Features**: 42 pieces, basic tools, emergency supplies, storage case
- **Why Mid-Range**: Good selection of tools, organized storage, reasonable price

Budget Choice: Basic Roadside Kit

- **Product**: AmazonBasics Roadside Emergency Kit
- **Supplier**: Amazon, basic automotive sections
- **Price**: $25-40 per kit
- **Features**: Jumper cables, basic tools, emergency triangle, gloves
- **Why Budget**: Covers essential needs, very affordable, and Amazon reliability

Bicycle Transportation
Premium Choice: Trek 4 Series Hybrid

- **Product**: Trek FX 3 Disc Hybrid Bicycle
- **Supplier**: Trek dealers, bicycle specialty shops
- **Price**: $700-900 per bicycle
- **Features**: Lightweight frame, disc brakes, 24-speed gearing
- **Why Premium**: Superior components, excellent warranty, dealer support

Mid-Range Choice: Giant Escape Series

- **Product**: Giant Escape 3 Hybrid Bike
- **Supplier**: Giant dealers, bicycle shops
- **Price**: $400-550 per bicycle
- **Features**: Aluminum frame, 21-speed, comfortable riding position
- **Why Mid-Range**: Good quality components, comfortable ride, competitive pricing

Budget Choice: Walmart Hybrid Bikes

- **Product**: Hyper 700C Men's/Women's Hybrid Bike
- **Supplier**: Walmart stores and website
- **Price**: $150-250 per bicycle
- **Features**: Basic components, 21-speed, includes basic accessories
- **Why Budget**: Very affordable, readily available, covers basic transportation needs

Supplier Directory & Purchasing Strategy
Premium Suppliers (High-Quality Focus)
REI Co-op

- **Specialties**: Outdoor equipment, camping gear, technical clothing
- **Why Choose**: Quality guarantee, member dividends, expert staff knowledge
- **Best For**: Shelter, clothing, outdoor cooking equipment, technical gear

Goal Zero

- **Specialties**: Portable power, solar equipment, charging solutions
- **Why Choose**: Innovation leader, excellent warranty, comprehensive ecosystem
- **Best For**: Power stations, solar panels, charging accessories

Adventure Medical Kits

- **Specialties**: Medical supplies, first aid kits, wilderness medicine
- **Why Choose**: Medical expertise, professional-grade supplies, comprehensive kits
- **Best For**: First aid supplies, medical equipment, emergency medical training

Mid-Range Suppliers (Value Focus)
Amazon

- **Specialties**: Everything, competitive pricing, fast delivery
- **Why Choose**: Convenience, customer reviews, return policy
- **Best For**: Comparison shopping, bulk purchases, hard-to-find items

Costco/Sam's Club

- **Specialties**: Bulk quantities, competitive pricing, quality brands
- **Why Choose**: Bulk discounts, quality guarantee, membership benefits
- **Best For**: Food storage, batteries, bulk supplies, major purchases

Home Depot/Lowe's

- **Specialties**: Tools, hardware, home improvement, generators
- **Why Choose**: Local availability, contractor pricing, tool rental
- **Best For**: Tools, hardware, generators, home fortification supplies

Budget Suppliers (Cost Focus)
Harbor Freight Tools

- **Specialties**: Affordable tools, hardware, automotive equipment
- **Why Choose**: Very low prices, frequent sales, basic quality adequate for many uses
- **Best For**: Basic hand tools, automotive equipment, shop supplies

Walmart

- **Specialties**: General merchandise, competitive pricing, nationwide availability
- **Why Choose**: Low prices, convenient locations, basic quality options
- **Best For**: Food storage, basic camping gear, personal care items

Dollar Tree/Family Dollar

- **Specialties**: Very low-cost items, basic supplies, personal care
- **Why Choose**: Extremely low prices, convenient locations
- **Best For**: Basic first aid supplies, personal hygiene, cleaning supplies

Purchasing Strategy Recommendations

Quality Investment Priorities: Invest in premium quality for items where failure could be life-threatening:

- **Medical supplies**: First aid kits, prescription medication storage
- **Water purification**: Primary water filtration systems
- **Communication equipment**: Primary two-way radios, emergency radios
- **Personal protection**: Pepper spray, tactical flashlights

Value Category Items: Choose mid-range options for frequently used items requiring reliability:

- **Tools**: Hand tools, multi-tools, basic repair equipment
- **Power equipment**: Battery chargers, portable power stations
- **Food storage**: Long-term food supplies, cooking equipment
- **Shelter**: Tents, sleeping bags, emergency clothing

Budget Category Items: Use budget options for backup items or where quality differences are minimal:

- **Storage containers**: Basic water storage, organization supplies
- **Personal care**: Hygiene supplies, cleaning materials
- **Basic supplies**: Batteries, flashlights, basic hardware
- **Documentation**: Storage binders, printing supplies

Bulk Purchasing & Group Buying

Community Group Purchases Organize neighborhood bulk purchases for better pricing on:

- **Food storage**: Rice, beans, canned goods in case quantities
- **Water storage**: Multiple families sharing shipping costs
- **Communication equipment**: Group purchases qualifying for volume discounts
- **Training**: Group training reducing per-person costs

Timing Purchases for Best Value

- **End of season sales**: Camping equipment, generators, winter gear
- **Black Friday/Cyber Monday**: Electronics, tools, major equipment purchases
- **Spring preparation**: Emergency supplies before storm season
- **Post-holiday clearance**: Batteries, flashlights, general supplies

Quality Assessment & Value Analysis
Determining True Value
Cost Per Use Analysis: Calculate long-term value rather than just initial purchase price:

- **High-use items**: Choose quality for items used frequently
- **Critical items**: Invest in reliability for life-safety equipment
- **Backup items**: Budget options acceptable for redundant supplies
- **Consumable items**: Balance quality with replacement frequency

Warranty & Support Considerations: Factor warranty and support into value calculations:

- **Premium brands**: Often include comprehensive warranties and customer support
- **Mid-range brands**: Usually offer reasonable warranties with good customer service
- **Budget brands**: Limited warranties but acceptable for non-critical applications

Reviews & Research Strategy: Make informed decisions using multiple information sources:

- **Professional reviews**: Outdoor magazines, preparedness publications
- **Customer reviews**: Amazon, REI customer feedback, forum discussions
- **Expert recommendations**: Emergency management professionals, first responders
- **Community feedback**: Local preparedness groups, neighbor experiences

This comprehensive supplier and product guide provides the foundation for making informed purchasing decisions that balance quality, functionality, and cost across all preparedness categories. Focus on premium quality for life-critical items while using budget options for backup supplies and non-essential items.

Appendix C

Seasonal Adjustment Checklists: Year-Round Preparedness Optimization

"Effective preparedness adapts to seasonal challenges and opportunities—strategic seasonal adjustments ensure your family's emergency systems perform optimally regardless of weather conditions, temperature extremes, or seasonal hazards."

Preparedness systems require regular seasonal adjustments to maintain peak effectiveness throughout the year. Weather patterns, temperature extremes, seasonal hazards, and changing daylight hours all impact emergency equipment performance and family needs. These comprehensive seasonal checklists ensure your preparedness systems remain optimized for current conditions while preparing for upcoming seasonal challenges.

Spring Preparedness Checklist (March - May)

Spring represents renewal and preparation—the optimal time for major system maintenance, equipment testing, and preparation for severe weather season.

System Maintenance & Equipment Testing
Water System Spring Maintenance

- [ ] **Rotate stored water**: Empty and refill all water storage containers
- [ ] **Test filtration systems**: Run water through all filters and check flow rates
- [ ] **Inspect storage containers**: Check for cracks, leaks, or algae growth

- [ ] **Clean rainwater collection**: Remove debris from gutters and collection surfaces
- [ ] **Test water purification**: Verify chemical purification tablets are not expired
- [ ] **Calibrate testing equipment**: Test pH meters, TDS meters, and water testing kits

Power System Spring Checkup

- [ ] **Solar panel cleaning**: Remove winter debris and clean solar panel surfaces
- [ ] **Battery testing**: Load test all batteries and replace weak units
- [ ] **Generator maintenance**: Change oil, replace air filter, test fuel system
- [ ] **Electrical connections**: Inspect and tighten all electrical connections
- [ ] **Inverter testing**: Test all power inverters under load conditions
- [ ] **Charge controller calibration**: Verify solar charge controllers are functioning properly

Communication System Updates

- [ ] **Radio programming**: Update frequencies and test all communication equipment
- [ ] **Battery replacement**: Replace batteries in all communication devices
- [ ] **Antenna inspection**: Check antenna connections and weather damage
- [ ] **Range testing**: Test the communication range from various locations
- [ ] **Emergency contacts**: Update emergency contact lists and phone numbers

Severe Weather Preparation

Spring Storm Season Preparation

- [ ] **Weather radio programming**: Program NOAA weather radio for local alerts
- [ ] **Storm shelter preparation**: Inspect and stock designated safe areas
- [ ] **Window protection materials**: Verify availability of plywood or storm shutters
- [ ] **Drainage systems**: Clear storm drains and inspect property drainage
- [ ] **Tree hazard assessment**: Remove dead branches and assess tree health
- [ ] **Insurance review**: Review homeowner's insurance and document the current property condition

Flood Preparation Systems

- [ ] **Flood barrier materials**: Inventory sandbags, plastic sheeting, and sealers
- [ ] **Sump pump testing**: Test sump pumps and backup power systems
- [ ] **Basement waterproofing**: Apply basement sealer and check foundation drainage
- [ ] **Important document protection**: Ensure critical documents are in waterproof storage
- [ ] **Evacuation route review**: Check flood evacuation routes and alternative paths

Tornado Preparedness

- [ ] **Safe room supplies**: Stock safe areas with water, food, and communication equipment
- [ ] **Emergency alert systems**: Test tornado sirens and smartphone alert systems
- [ ] **Family drill practice**: Conduct tornado drills with timing and route evaluation

- [ ] **Structural reinforcement**: Inspect and reinforce safe room doors and anchoring
- [ ] **Emergency kit accessibility**: Ensure emergency supplies are accessible from safe areas

Spring Supply Rotation & Restocking
Food System Spring Management

- [ ] **Expiration date audit**: Check all food supplies for approaching expiration dates
- [ ] **Inventory rotation**: Move older items to the front, newer items to the back
- [ ] **Bulk food transfer**: Transfer bulk foods to smaller containers for rotation
- [ ] **Menu planning**: Plan meals using older stored foods to maintain freshness
- [ ] **Garden preparation**: Start an emergency food garden and plant fruit trees

Medical Supply Spring Review

- [ ] **Prescription refills**: Ensure all prescription medications have adequate supplies
- [ ] **First aid kit restocking**: Replace used items and check expiration dates
- [ ] **Medical equipment testing**: Test blood pressure cuffs, thermometers, and monitoring equipment
- [ ] **Allergy season preparation**: Stock antihistamines and allergy medications
- [ ] **Sun protection supplies**: Restock sunscreen, insect repellent, and protective clothing

Summer Preparedness Checklist (June - August)

Summer brings heat stress, drought conditions, wildfire risk, and hurricane season—requiring specialized preparations for temperature extremes and seasonal hazards.

Heat Emergency Preparation
Cooling System Optimization

- [ ] **Air conditioning maintenance**: Clean filters, check refrigerant, test backup power
- [ ] **Fan inventory**: Test all fans and ensure backup cooling methods are available
- [ ] **Cooling center locations**: Identify public cooling centers and backup cooling options
- [ ] **Heat illness prevention**: Stock electrolyte supplements and cooling towels
- [ ] **Vehicle cooling systems**: Check vehicle air conditioning and cooling system maintenance
- [ ] **Pet cooling preparations**: Prepare cooling mats, extra water, and shade structures for pets

Water Management for Heat

- [ ] **Increased water storage**: Expand water storage for increased consumption during heat
- [ ] **Ice production**: Ensure adequate ice-making and storage capability
- [ ] **Swimming pool maintenance**: Maintain pool water quality for emergency cooling
- [ ] **Sprinkler system testing**: Test irrigation systems for cooling and fire protection
- [ ] **Hydration monitoring**: Establish hydration schedules and monitoring for family members

Wildfire Preparation Systems
Defensible Space Creation

APPENDIX C

- [ ] **Vegetation management**: Clear brush and dry vegetation within 100 feet of structures
- [ ] **Irrigation system expansion**: Install sprinkler systems for structure protection
- [ ] **Fire-resistant landscaping**: Plant fire-resistant plants and create fuel breaks
- [ ] **Roof and gutter cleaning**: Remove flammable debris from roof and gutters
- [ ] **Access route maintenance**: Ensure emergency vehicle access and escape routes are clear

Wildfire Emergency Equipment

- [ ] **Fire suppression tools**: Stock fire extinguishers, hoses, and suppression equipment
- [ ] **Air filtration systems**: Prepare high-efficiency air filters for smoke protection
- [ ] **Evacuation preparation**: Pack go-bags with fire-specific evacuation supplies
- [ ] **Structure protection**: Install metal screens over vents and attic openings
- [ ] **Emergency communication**: Establish communication plans with neighbors and authorities

Hurricane & Tropical Storm Preparation
Hurricane Season System Preparation

- [ ] **Storm tracking tools**: Set up hurricane tracking apps and weather monitoring
- [ ] **Window protection**: Install or prepare hurricane shutters and boarding materials
- [ ] **Generator preparation**: Test generators, fuel systems, and load management

- [ ] **Water storage expansion**: Increase water storage capacity for extended outages
- [ ] **Evacuation planning**: Review evacuation routes and destination planning

Flood Protection Systems

- [ ] **Sandbag preparation**: Acquire sandbags and flood barrier materials
- [ ] **Drainage system maintenance**: Clean storm drains and check property drainage
- [ ] **Important item elevation**: Move valuable items to higher levels of the home
- [ ] **Sump pump systems**: Test and maintain all water removal equipment
- [ ] **Insurance documentation**: Document property condition with photos and video

Summer Supply Adjustments
Heat-Specific Supply Management

- [ ] **Electrolyte supplements**: Stock sports drinks, electrolyte powders, and salt tablets
- [ ] **Cooling supplies**: Acquire cooling towels, spray bottles, and portable misting systems
- [ ] **Sun protection gear**: Stock wide-brim hats, UV-protective clothing, and high-SPF sunscreen
- [ ] **Heat illness treatment**: Prepare ice packs, cooling blankets, and heat exhaustion treatment supplies
- [ ] **Food safety management**: Emphasize food safety during high temperatures and power outages

Fall Preparedness Checklist (September - November)

Fall preparation focuses on winterization, heating system preparation, and capitalizing on harvest season opportunities while preparing for colder weather.

Winter Preparation Systems
Heating System Winterization

- [ ] **Furnace maintenance**: Clean or replace filters, test heating system operation
- [ ] **Chimney cleaning**: Clean and inspect chimney and fireplace systems
- [ ] **Backup heating preparation**: Test space heaters, wood stoves, and alternative heating
- [ ] **Insulation inspection**: Check attic, wall, and basement insulation for gaps
- [ ] **Weather stripping replacement**: Replace worn weather stripping around doors and windows

Cold Weather Equipment Testing

- [ ] **Winter clothing inspection**: Check winter coats, boots, gloves, and cold-weather gear
- [ ] **Vehicle winterization**: Test heating systems, check antifreeze, and prepare winter vehicle kit
- [ ] **Pipe insulation**: Insulate exposed pipes and outdoor faucets for freeze protection
- [ ] **Roof and gutter maintenance**: Clean gutters, check roof condition, remove debris
- [ ] **Generator cold weather preparation**: Test cold weather starting and winter fuel additives

Food Preservation & Harvest Season
Harvest Season Food Preservation

- [ ] **Canning equipment preparation**: Test pressure canners, replace

gaskets, calibrate gauges
- [ ] **Dehydration systems**: Clean and test food dehydrators and drying equipment
- [ ] **Freezing preparation**: Deep clean freezers and organize for harvest season preservation
- [ ] **Root cellar preparation**: Prepare cold storage areas for winter vegetable storage
- [ ] **Bulk food purchasing**: Take advantage of harvest season pricing for bulk food purchases

Garden Winterization

- [ ] **Final harvest**: Harvest remaining vegetables and prepare for winter storage
- [ ] **Seed collection**: Collect and properly store seeds for next year's garden
- [ ] **Soil preparation**: Add compost and prepare garden beds for winter
- [ ] **Tool maintenance**: Clean, sharpen, and store garden tools for winter
- [ ] **Irrigation system winterization**: Drain and winterize irrigation systems to prevent freeze damage

Emergency Lighting Preparation
Reduced Daylight Preparation

- [ ] **Battery replacement**: Replace batteries in all flashlights and lanterns
- [ ] **Emergency lighting testing**: Test all emergency lighting systems and backup power
- [ ] **Solar light maintenance**: Clean and test solar-powered lighting systems
- [ ] **Candle safety preparation**: Stock emergency candles and review candle safety procedures
- [ ] **Generator lighting capability**: Test generator capacity for essential lighting needs

Winter Preparedness Checklist (December - February)

Winter preparedness emphasizes heating, transportation, and severe weather response while managing the challenges of cold temperatures and limited daylight.

Cold Weather Emergency Systems
Heating System Optimization

- [ ] **Primary heating maintenance**: Monitor heating system performance and fuel levels
- [ ] **Backup heating systems**: Test space heaters, generators, and alternative heating sources
- [ ] **Fuel storage management**: Maintain adequate fuel supplies for heating systems
- [ ] **Carbon monoxide safety**: Test CO detectors and ensure proper ventilation
- [ ] **Heating distribution**: Optimize heating distribution throughout living areas

Insulation & Weather Protection

- [ ] **Draft elimination**: Seal air leaks around windows, doors, and other openings
- [ ] **Pipe freeze protection**: Monitor pipe temperatures and maintain adequate heat
- [ ] **Attic ventilation**: Ensure proper attic ventilation to prevent ice dams
- [ ] **Emergency heating areas**: Designate and prepare emergency heating areas for power outages
- [ ] **Cold weather clothing**: Organize and maintain cold weather clothing for all family members

Winter Storm Preparedness
Snow & Ice Storm Preparation

- [ ] **Snow removal equipment**: Test snow blowers, maintain shovels, and ice melt supplies
- [ ] **Vehicle winter equipment**: Check tire chains, winter tires, and vehicle winter kit
- [ ] **Power outage preparation**: Prepare for extended power outages during ice storms
- [ ] **Food storage protection**: Protect food storage from freezing temperatures
- [ ] **Communication during storms**: Prepare communication equipment for storm conditions

Blizzard Emergency Systems

- [ ] **Extended supply verification**: Ensure adequate supplies for multi-day isolation
- [ ] **Alternative cooking methods**: Prepare non-electric cooking methods for power outages
- [ ] **Water system freeze protection**: Protect water storage and plumbing from freezing
- [ ] **Emergency shelter heating**: Prepare heating for emergency shelter areas
- [ ] **Family emergency drills**: Practice winter emergency procedures and shelter-in-place

Winter Equipment Maintenance
Cold Weather Equipment Care

- [ ] **Battery performance monitoring**: Monitor battery performance in cold temperatures
- [ ] **Generator winter operation**: Test generator cold weather starting and operation
- [ ] **Vehicle emergency kit updates**: Update vehicle kits with winter-specific supplies

- [ ] **Communication equipment cold testing**: Test radio and communication equipment in cold
- [ ] **Tool winterization**: Prepare tools and equipment for cold-weather operation

Monthly Maintenance Schedule
Every Month, Year-Round Tasks
System Status Verification

- [ ] **Battery testing**: Test smoke detectors, CO detectors, and emergency equipment batteries
- [ ] **Water storage inspection**: Visual inspection of water storage containers for leaks or contamination
- [ ] **Food expiration monitoring**: Check approaching expiration dates and plan usage
- [ ] **Communication equipment testing**: Test all radios and communication devices
- [ ] **Emergency kit accessibility**: Verify emergency supplies are accessible and organized

Documentation & Planning Updates

- [ ] **Contact information updates**: Verify emergency contact information is current
- [ ] **Insurance policy review**: Review insurance coverage and update as needed
- [ ] **Family emergency plan review**: Practice emergency procedures and update plans
- [ ] **Supply inventory tracking**: Update inventory records and reorder depleted supplies
- [ ] **Weather monitoring**: Monitor seasonal weather patterns and adjust preparations

Quarterly Deep Maintenance Tasks
Comprehensive System Testing

- [ ] **Generator load testing**: Full load test of generators and backup power systems
- [ ] **Water filtration flow testing**: Test filtration systems under full load conditions
- [ ] **Medical equipment calibration**: Test blood pressure cuffs, thermometers, and monitoring equipment
- [ ] **Communication range testing**: Test radio communication from various distances and locations
- [ ] **Emergency drill execution**: Conduct comprehensive family emergency drills

Equipment Rotation & Replacement

- [ ] **Seasonal supply rotation**: Rotate seasonal supplies and update for current weather conditions
- [ ] **Bulk supply rotation**: Rotate bulk stored supplies using first-in-first-out principles
- [ ] **Equipment wear assessment**: Inspect equipment for wear and plan replacement schedule
- [ ] **Technology updates**: Update communication equipment, programming, and software
- [ ] **Insurance and warranty tracking**: Monitor equipment warranties and insurance coverage

Regional Climate Adaptations
Hot Climate Adjustments (Southwest, Southeast)
Year-Round Hot Weather Considerations

- [ ] **Enhanced cooling systems**: Prioritize cooling over heating systems and supplies

- [ ] **UV protection emphasis**: Stock high-SPF sunscreen, UV-protective clothing, wide-brim hats
- [ ] **Heat illness prevention**: Emphasize electrolyte replacement and heat illness recognition
- [ ] **Water consumption planning**: Increase water storage and consumption calculations for heat
- [ ] **Food safety focus**: Emphasize food safety and spoilage prevention in high temperatures

Cold Climate Adjustments (Northern States, Mountains)
Extended Winter Preparation

- [ ] **Extended heating fuel supplies**: Plan for longer heating seasons and greater fuel consumption
- [ ] **Enhanced insulation systems**: Prioritize building insulation and heat retention
- [ ] **Cold weather equipment emphasis**: Focus on cold weather clothing, heating, and vehicle preparation
- [ ] **Extended food storage**: Plan for longer periods of limited food access during winter storms
- [ ] **Daylight compensation**: Prepare for extended periods of limited daylight

Coastal Climate Adjustments (Atlantic, Pacific, Gulf Coasts)
Hurricane and Storm Surge Preparation

- [ ] **Wind protection systems**: Emphasize hurricane shutters, roof reinforcement, and wind protection
- [ ] **Flood protection planning**: Plan for storm surge, coastal flooding, and saltwater intrusion
- [ ] **Evacuation emphasis**: Focus on evacuation planning and transportation readiness
- [ ] **Saltwater equipment protection**: Protect equipment from saltwa-

ter corrosion and damage
- [ ] **Extended power outage planning**: Plan for extended power outages following major storms

Earthquake Zone Adjustments (West Coast, New Madrid)
Seismic Event Preparation

- [ ] **Structural reinforcement**: Secure water heaters, tall furniture, and heavy objects
- [ ] **Emergency access preparation**: Prepare for blocked exits and damaged infrastructure
- [ ] **Utility shutoff preparation**: Learn utility shutoff procedures and keep tools accessible
- [ ] **Glass protection planning**: Prepare for broken glass and window damage
- [ ] **Communication system hardening**: Prepare for damaged communication infrastructure

Emergency Seasonal Transitions
Unexpected Weather Events
Rapid Weather Changes When weather patterns change rapidly or extreme events occur outside normal seasons:

- [ ] **Rapid supply adjustment**: Quickly adjust supplies for unexpected weather conditions
- [ ] **Equipment reallocation**: Move seasonal equipment to accessible locations
- [ ] **Communication updates**: Update family and community about changing conditions
- [ ] **Transportation adjustments**: Modify transportation plans for unexpected weather
- [ ] **Utility system adaptation**: Adjust heating, cooling, and power systems for conditions

Climate Change Adaptations

Evolving Weather Patterns. As climate patterns change, seasonal preparations must adapt:

- [ ] **Historical data updates**: Update preparations based on recent weather patterns rather than historical norms
- [ ] **Extreme event planning**: Prepare for more frequent extreme weather events
- [ ] **Season shift planning**: Adapt to shifting seasonal timing and duration
- [ ] **Infrastructure stress planning**: Plan for increased stress on utilities and infrastructure
- [ ] **Community coordination**: Coordinate with the community on changing seasonal challenges

Seasonal Preparedness Integration
Family Coordination
Seasonal Responsibility Assignment

- [ ] **Seasonal task assignment**: Assign family members specific seasonal preparedness responsibilities
- [ ] **Seasonal training updates**: Update family training based on upcoming seasonal hazards
- [ ] **Seasonal drill scheduling**: Schedule seasonal-specific emergency drills and practice
- [ ] **Seasonal supply education**: Educate family members about seasonal supply changes and locations
- [ ] **Seasonal communication planning**: Update communication plans for seasonal challenges

Community Integration
Neighborhood Seasonal Coordination

- [ ] **Community seasonal planning**: Coordinate seasonal preparations with neighbors and the community
- [ ] **Shared resource seasonal management**: Plan seasonal sharing of community resources and equipment
- [ ] **Community seasonal drills**: Participate in community-wide seasonal emergency drills
- [ ] **Seasonal mutual aid planning**: Update mutual aid agreements for seasonal challenges
- [ ] **Community seasonal communication**: Maintain communication about seasonal preparations and challenges

Chapter Summary: Optimizing Year-Round Preparedness

Seasonal adjustment checklists ensure your family's preparedness systems remain optimized for current conditions while preparing for upcoming challenges. By implementing systematic seasonal adjustments, you'll have:

✓ **Weather-optimized systems** that perform effectively in current seasonal conditions

✓ **Proactive hazard preparation** that anticipates and prepares for seasonal threats

✓ **Equipment longevity** through proper seasonal maintenance and care

✓ **Cost-effective supply management** that minimizes waste through proper rotation

✓ **Family safety optimization** that adapts protection strategies to seasonal risks

✓ **Community coordination** that aligns family preparations with community seasonal needs

Implementation Benefits:

- **Maintained system effectiveness**: Regular maintenance ensures all systems perform when needed
- **Seasonal hazard readiness**: Specific preparation for seasonal threats like hurricanes, blizzards, and wildfires
- **Equipment longevity**: Proper seasonal care extends equipment life

and reliability
- **Supply optimization**: Rotation and seasonal adjustments minimize waste and maximize freshness
- **Cost management**: Seasonal purchasing and maintenance spreads costs throughout the year

Key Success Factors:

- **Consistent scheduling**: Use calendar reminders for seasonal tasks and maintenance
- **Regional adaptation**: Customize seasonal preparations for local climate and hazards
- **Family participation**: Include all family members in seasonal preparation activities
- **Community coordination**: Align seasonal preparations with neighbors and community efforts
- **Continuous improvement**: Adapt seasonal routines based on experience and changing conditions

Long-Term Benefits: Systematic seasonal preparedness creates an improved capability over time:

- **Institutional knowledge**: Family develops a deep understanding of seasonal preparation needs
- **Equipment mastery**: Regular maintenance builds expertise with all preparedness equipment
- **Community integration**: Seasonal coordination builds stronger community relationships
- **Cost optimization**: Understanding seasonal patterns enables better purchasing timing
- **Risk reduction**: Proactive seasonal preparation reduces family vulnerability to seasonal hazards

Seasonal preparedness represents the difference between static supply accumulation and dynamic, responsive preparedness that adapts to changing conditions while maintaining peak effectiveness throughout the year.

Appendix D

Budget-Phased Implementation Timeline: Building Comprehensive Preparedness Over Time

"Comprehensive preparedness doesn't require massive upfront investment—strategic phased implementation spreads costs over time while building capability systematically, ensuring every dollar spent provides maximum family security."

Building comprehensive family preparedness can seem financially overwhelming when viewed as a single large investment. This phased implementation timeline breaks preparedness development into manageable monthly investments that build systematically toward complete family resilience while respecting budget constraints and cash flow limitations. Each phase prioritizes life-critical needs first while building toward advanced capability over time.

Implementation Philosophy & Budgeting Strategy
Total Cost Overview
Complete Preparedness Investment Ranges:

- **Basic Preparedness** (Essential survival capability): $8,000-15,000
- **Comprehensive Preparedness** (All 14 chapters): $15,000-30,000
- **Advanced Preparedness** (Premium equipment + technology): $25,000-50,000

Monthly Investment Options:

- **Budget Track**: $200-400/month over 36 months = $7,200-14,400 total
- **Standard Track**: $400-800/month over 24 months = $9,600-19,200 total
- **Accelerated Track**: $800-1,500/month over 12 months = $9,600-18,000 total

Phasing Principles
Priority-Based Implementation:

1. **Life-Critical Systems First**: Water, food, medical, shelter
2. **Security & Communication**: Protection and coordination capability
3. **Optimization & Advanced Systems**: Technology integration and community building
4. **Premium Upgrades**: Quality improvements and advanced capability

Budget Management Strategies:

- **Start small, build consistently**: $200/month minimum commitment
- **Seasonal purchasing optimization**: Time purchases around sales and seasonal needs
- **Group buying opportunities**: Community purchasing for better pricing
- **DIY vs. purchase analysis**: Build vs. buy decisions for maximum value

Phase 1: Foundation Survival Systems (Months 1-6)
Priority: Basic survival capability for family of four Investment: $200-400/month | Total: $1,200-2,400

Month 1: Water Security Foundation ($200-350)
Essential Water Systems (Chapter 1)
Week 1: Basic Water Storage ($75-125)

- 4 × 7-gallon Aquatainer containers = $100-140

APPENDIX D

- Or 2 × 55-gallon food-grade barrels = $90-150

Week 2: Water Purification Basics ($50-75)

- 200 water purification tablets = $15-25
- 1 gallon unscented bleach = $3-5
- 4 LifeStraw personal filters = $60-80

Week 3: Water Storage Setup ($40-80)

- Storage area preparation and organization
- Spigot and funnel accessories = $15-25
- Water rotation labeling system = $10-20

Week 4: Water Testing & Documentation ($35-70)

- Water testing kit = $20-40
- Storage documentation system = $10-15
- Initial water fill and system test = $5-15

Month 1 Capability: 14-day water supply with basic purification
Month 2: Food Storage Foundation ($250-400)
Basic Food Security (Chapter 2)
Week 1: Protein Foundation ($80-120)

- 20 cans of tuna (5 oz) = $30-50
- 20 cans of chicken (5 oz) = $40-60
- 10 cans of beans (15 oz) = $10-20

Week 2: Ready-to-Eat Meals ($100-150)

- 15 MREs (variety pack) = $120-180
- Or 15 freeze-dried meals = $90-135

Week 3: High-Energy Snacks ($40-80)

- 30 granola bars = $15-30
- 5 lbs mixed nuts = $25-50
- 2 lbs dried fruit = $10-20

Week 4: Cooking Equipment ($30-50)

- Manual can openers (2) = $10-20
- Portable camp stove + fuel = $50-80
- Or emergency fuel tablets = $15-25

Month 2 Capability: 7-day food supply with cooking capability
Month 3: Medical Preparedness ($150-300)
Essential Medical Systems (Chapter 3)
Week 1: First Aid Kit Foundation ($50-100)

- Comprehensive first aid kit = $60-120
- Or build a custom kit with generic supplies = $25-50

Week 2: Prescription Management ($40-80)

- 14-day prescription backup = Variable cost
- Pill organizers and storage = $20-40

Week 3: OTC Medicine Cabinet ($30-60)

- Pain relievers (ibuprofen, acetaminophen) = $15-30
- Antihistamines and antidiarrheals = $10-20
- Thermometer and basic medical supplies = $15-30

Week 4: Special Medical Needs ($30-60)

- Family-specific medical supplies
- Medical information documentation = $10-20

Month 3 Capability: Complete medical care for minor injuries and illnesses

Month 4: Basic Tools & Repair ($200-400)
Essential Tool Systems (Chapter 4)

Week 1: Multi-Tools & Knives ($40-120)

- 2 quality multi-tools = $80-200
- Or 1 premium + 1 budget multi-tool = $60-120

Week 2: Hand Tool Basics ($80-150)

- Hammer, screwdrivers, adjustable wrenches = $50-100
- Pliers set and cutting tools = $30-50

Week 3: Fasteners & Repair Materials ($40-80)

- Nails, screws, nuts, and bolts assortment = $25-50
- Duct tape, zip ties, paracord = $15-30

Week 4: Storage & Organization ($40-50)

- Tool storage and organization system = $30-80

Month 4 Capability: Basic repair and maintenance capability

Month 5: Power & Communication ($200-500)
Basic Power Systems (Chapter 5)

Week 1: Lighting Systems ($50-100)

- 4 LED flashlights = $40-120
- 4 headlamps = $25-100

- Lanterns and emergency lighting = $30-80

Week 2: Battery Systems ($60-120)

- Battery inventory (AA, AAA, C, D, 9V) = $40-80
- Battery charger and rechargeable batteries = $40-80

Week 3: Communication Equipment ($80-200)

- 4 two-way radios = $80-200
- NOAA weather radio = $30-60
- Emergency communication accessories = $20-40

Week 4: Basic Power Generation ($150-300)

- 4 power banks (20,000 mAh each) = $160-320
- Or smaller generator = $200-400

Month 5 Capability: Emergency lighting and basic communication
Month 6: Shelter & Warmth ($250-450)
Basic Shelter Systems (Chapter 6)
Week 1: Emergency Shelter ($150-300)

- 4-person emergency tent = $100-400
- Or heavy-duty tarps and rope = $50-100

Week 2: Sleeping Systems ($150-300)

- 4 sleeping bags (temperature appropriate) = $120-400
- 4 sleeping pads = $60-200

Week 3: Clothing & Weather Protection ($100-200)

- Base layer clothing sets = $80-160
- Weather protection (rain gear, warm layers) = $80-200

Week 4: Heating Equipment ($100-200)

- Emergency heating system (safe indoor heater) = $100-200
- Hand warmers and heat retention supplies = $20-40

Month 6 Capability: Complete shelter and warmth for a family of four
Phase 1 Total Investment: $1,250-2,700 **Phase 1 Capability**: Basic 7-14 day survival for all essential needs
Phase 2: Comprehensive Protection Systems (Months 7-12)
Priority: Security, sanitation, documentation, special needs Investment: $300-600/month | Total: $1,800-3,600
Month 7: Hygiene & Sanitation ($200-400)
Complete Sanitation Systems (Chapter 7)
Week 1: Personal Hygiene Systems ($50-100)

- 3-month supply personal hygiene items = $50-100
- Water-efficient hygiene supplies = $30-60

Week 2: Waste Management ($75-150)

- Portable toilet system = $60-120
- Waste bags and sanitation supplies = $30-60
- Odor control and cleaning supplies = $20-40

Week 3: Cleaning & Disinfection ($40-80)

- Disinfectants and cleaning supplies = $30-60
- Cleaning tools and equipment = $20-40

Week 4: Laundry Systems ($50-100)

- Manual laundry equipment = $40-80
- Clothesline and drying supplies = $20-40

Month 8: Documentation & Financial ($300-600)
Document Protection Systems (Chapter 8)
Week 1: Physical Document Protection ($100-200)

- Fireproof document safe = $100-300
- Document organization system = $50-100

Week 2: Digital Backup Systems ($150-300)

- Encrypted USB drives and cloud storage = $100-200
- Document scanning and digital organization = $50-100

Week 3: Emergency Cash & Financial ($200-400)

- Emergency cash reserves ($500-1,000) = Face value
- Prepaid cards and alternative payment methods = $50-200

Week 4: Insurance & Legal Documents ($50-150)

- Legal document review and updates = $100-500
- Insurance documentation and updates = $50-200

Month 9: Special Needs Systems ($200-600)
Vulnerable Population Support (Chapter 9)
Week 1: Child/Infant Needs ($100-300)

- Infant formula and feeding supplies = $100-200
- Child safety and comfort items = $50-150

Week 2: Senior Support Systems ($100-300)

- Enhanced medication management = $50-150
- Mobility and accessibility aids = $100-300

Week 3: Pet Preparedness ($100-250)

- 14-day pet food supply = $50-150
- Pet emergency equipment and supplies = $50-100

Week 4: Medical Condition Management ($150-400)

- Chronic disease management supplies = Variable
- Specialized medical equipment = $100-500

Month 10: Security & Self-Defense ($200-500)
Protection Systems (Chapter 10)

Week 1: Personal Protection ($100-200)

- Pepper spray for family members = $50-100
- Personal alarms and tactical flashlights = $50-150

Week 2: Home Security ($150-400)

- Door reinforcement and security hardware = $100-300
- Window protection and security film = $100-300

Week 3: Fire Safety Systems ($100-250)

- Fire extinguishers and smoke detectors = $75-200
- Fire escape equipment and planning = $50-150

Week 4: Security Training ($100-300)

- Self-defense training for family = $200-600

- Security system setup and testing = $50-100

Month 11: Transportation & Evacuation ($300-700)
Mobility Systems (Chapter 11)
Week 1: Vehicle Emergency Equipment ($150-400)

- Vehicle emergency kit and tools = $100-250
- Fuel storage and management = $75-200

Week 2: Evacuation Supplies ($200-500)

- Go-bags for each family member = $150-400
- Evacuation equipment and supplies = $100-300

Week 3: Alternative Transportation ($200-500)

- Bicycles or transportation backup = $300-800
- Transportation safety equipment = $50-150

Week 4: Evacuation Planning ($50-150)

- Route planning and navigation equipment = $100-250
- Destination planning and coordination = $50-150

Month 12: Planning & Skills Development ($200-500)
Coordination Systems (Chapter 12)
Week 1: Family Planning Systems ($50-150)

- Emergency plan development and documentation = $50-100
- Communication system setup = $100-250

Week 2: Skills Training Investment ($150-400)

- CPR/First Aid certification = $100-200 per person
- Technical skills training = $100-300

Week 3: Community Integration ($50-200)

- Community preparedness participation = Variable
- Mutual aid system development = $50-150

Week 4: Equipment Training ($100-200)

- Family equipment training and practice = Time investment
- System testing and optimization = $50-150

Phase 2 Total Investment: $1,800-4,200 **Phase 2 Capability**: Comprehensive preparedness with security and advanced systems

Phase 3: Advanced Systems & Optimization (Months 13-18)

Priority: Technology integration, community building, advanced capability
Investment: $400-800/month | Total: $2,400-4,800

Month 13: Resource Optimization & Technology ($400-800)
Advanced Management Systems (Chapter 13)

Week 1: Digital Inventory Management ($100-200)

- Inventory management software and equipment = $100-300
- Barcode scanning and tracking systems = $100-250

Week 2: Smart Home Integration ($200-500)

- IoT sensors and monitoring equipment = $200-600
- Automated control systems = $200-500

Week 3: Advanced Communication ($200-400)

- Amateur radio equipment and licensing = $300-800

- Mesh networking and advanced systems = $200-600

Week 4: Community Resource Networks ($100-300)

- Community platform participation = $50-200
- Shared resource system development = $100-300

Month 14: Advanced Power Systems ($500-1,000)
Power Independence (Chapter 14)

Week 1: Solar Power Systems ($300-600)

- Portable solar panels and charge controllers = $300-800
- Battery bank expansion = $200-600

Week 2: Advanced Power Management ($200-500)

- Power monitoring and management systems = $200-500
- Grid-tie and backup power integration = $300-800

Week 3: Alternative Power Generation ($200-400)

- Hand-crank and mechanical power systems = $100-300
- Backup generator upgrade or addition = $400-1,000

Week 4: Power System Integration ($100-300)

- Electrical system integration and safety = $200-500
- Power system optimization and testing = $100-200

Month 15: Advanced Water Systems ($300-600)
Water Independence (Chapter 14)

Week 1: Water Production Systems ($200-500)

- Well pump or advanced filtration = $300-1,000
- Rainwater collection enhancement = $200-600

Week 2: Water Treatment & Recycling ($200-400)

- Advanced water treatment systems = $200-600
- Greywater recycling systems = $300-800

Week 3: Water Storage Expansion ($100-300)

- Large-scale water storage systems = $200-600
- Water distribution and pressure systems = $200-500

Week 4: Water System Integration ($100-200)

- System integration and automation = $100-400
- Water quality monitoring = $100-300

Month 16: Food Production Systems ($300-700)
Sustainable Food Systems (Chapter 14)

Week 1: Garden Establishment ($200-500)

- Garden setup, soil improvement, tools = $200-600
- Greenhouse or season extension = $300-1,000

Week 2: Food Preservation Equipment ($200-500)

- Canning equipment and pressure canners = $150-400
- Dehydrators and preservation systems = $200-500

Week 3: Livestock Systems ($200-600)

- Poultry setup (chickens for eggs) = $300-800

- Small livestock systems if applicable = $500-1,500

Week 4: Food Processing Equipment ($150-300)

- Grain mills, food processors = $200-600
- Value-added processing equipment = $200-500

Month 17: Economic Resilience ($200-600)
Financial Independence Systems (Chapter 14)
Week 1: Alternative Investments ($200-500)

- Precious metals starter investment = $300-1,000
- Alternative asset research and acquisition = Variable

Week 2: Local Currency & Trade ($100-300)

- Community currency participation = $100-500
- Barter network development = $50-200

Week 3: Business Development ($200-500)

- Emergency-related business setup = $300-1,000
- Service business development = $200-800

Week 4: Financial System Integration ($100-300)

- Financial planning and optimization = $200-600
- Economic resilience planning = $100-400

Month 18: Community & Leadership ($200-500)
Community Resilience (Chapter 14)
Week 1: Leadership Development ($200-400)

- Leadership training and development = $300-800
- Community organizing skills = $200-500

Week 2: Community Projects ($200-600)

- Community preparedness projects = $300-1,000
- Shared resource development = $200-700

Week 3: Knowledge Systems ($100-300)

- Knowledge preservation and documentation = $100-300
- Teaching and training system development = $150-400

Week 4: Long-term Planning ($100-300)

- Multi-generational planning systems = $100-400
- Community sustainability projects = $200-800

Phase 3 Total Investment: $2,800-6,600 **Phase 3 Capability**: Advanced preparedness with technology integration and community leadership

Phase 4: Premium Upgrades & Mastery (Months 19-24)

Priority: Premium equipment upgrades, advanced training, system optimization Investment: $500-1,000/month | Total: $3,000-6,000

Months 19-20: Equipment Upgrades ($1,000-2,000)
Premium System Replacements

Equipment Quality Upgrades:

- Replace budget items with premium equivalents = $800-1,500
- Add redundancy to critical systems = $600-1,200
- Professional-grade tool upgrades = $400-1,000
- Advanced medical equipment = $300-800

Months 21-22: Advanced Training & Skills ($800-1,500)

Professional Development
Advanced Training Programs:

- Wilderness medicine certification = $500-1,200
- Advanced amateur radio licensing = $200-500
- Leadership and emergency management = $500-1,500
- Technical skills development = $300-1,000

Months 23-24: System Integration & Optimization ($1,200-2,500)
Professional-Grade Integration
Complete System Integration:

- Home automation and monitoring = $800-2,000
- Professional communication systems = $1,000-3,000
- Advanced power and water systems = $1,500-5,000
- Community leadership systems = $500-1,500

Phase 4 Total Investment: $3,000-6,000 **Phase 4 Capability**: Professional-grade preparedness with advanced systems

Budget Management Strategies
Financing Options
Payment Strategies:

- **Monthly budgeting**: Set aside a consistent monthly amount
- **Seasonal purchasing**: Time purchases around sales and seasonal needs
- **Tax refund allocation**: Use annual tax refunds for major purchases
- **Bonus/windfall allocation**: Direct unexpected income to preparedness

Cost Reduction Techniques
Money-Saving Approaches:

- **Group buying**: Organize community bulk purchases

- **DIY construction**: Build vs. buy for appropriate items
- **Used equipment**: Quality used equipment for non-critical items
- **Seasonal sales**: Time purchases for maximum discount
- **Generic alternatives**: Generic supplies where quality differences are minimal

Priority Flexibility
Adaptation Strategies:

- **Threat-based prioritization**: Adjust priorities based on local threats
- **Budget constraints**: Scale back quantities while maintaining capabilities
- **Found opportunities**: Take advantage of unexpected deals and opportunities
- **Family changes**: Adapt priorities based on changing family needs

Return on Investment
Value Maximization:

- **Multi-use prioritization**: Choose equipment serving multiple functions
- **Quality investment**: Spend more on items used frequently or critical for safety
- **Training emphasis**: Invest in skills that multiply equipment effectiveness
- **Community benefits**: Choose investments that strengthen community relationships

Implementation Success Factors
Commitment & Consistency
Success Requirements:

- **Monthly budget discipline**: Consistent monthly investment regard-

less of other expenses
- **Priority maintenance**: Resist temptation to redirect preparedness funds to other purposes
- **Family buy-in**: Ensure all family members support and participate in preparedness building
- **Long-term perspective**: Focus on long-term capability rather than short-term convenience

Progress Tracking
Measurement Systems:

- **Capability tracking**: Document preparedness capabilities gained each month
- **Investment tracking**: Track total investment and cost-per-capability ratios
- **Skill development**: Document training completed and competencies gained
- **System testing**: Regular testing to ensure investments provide the expected capability

Adaptation & Flexibility
Responsive Implementation:

- **Threat changes**: Adapt priorities based on changing threat assessment
- **Budget changes**: Adjust timeline and priorities based on budget changes
- **Family changes**: Modify priorities based on changing family needs
- **Community opportunities**: Take advantage of community preparedness initiatives

Chapter Summary: Building Preparedness Within Budget Constraints

Budget-phased implementation transforms overwhelming preparedness costs into manageable monthly investments that build comprehensive family resilience over time. By implementing systematic budget-phased development, you'll have:

✓ **Manageable monthly investments** spreading costs over 12-24 months

✓ **Priority-based development** ensuring life-critical capabilities come first

✓ **Flexible budget options** accommodating different family financial situations

✓ **Progressive capability building** with each phase adding meaningful capability

✓ **Community integration opportunities,** reducing individual costs through group purchasing

✓ **Long-term affordability** makes comprehensive preparedness accessible to most families

Implementation Benefits:

- **Financial sustainability**: Monthly payments fit within normal family budgets
- **Immediate capability**: Each month adds meaningful preparedness capability
- **Reduced financial stress**: Avoids large upfront investments or debt accumulation
- **Flexibility**: Adaptation for changing family needs and budget constraints
- **Community benefits**: Group purchasing and shared resources reduce individual costs

Key Success Factors:

- **Consistent commitment**: Regular monthly investment regardless of other financial pressures
- **Priority discipline**: Maintain focus on life-critical needs before

convenience items
- **Quality balance**: Invest appropriately in quality where it matters most
- **Community integration**: Leverage group purchasing and shared resources for better value
- **Long-term perspective**: Focus on building lasting capability rather than accumulating supplies

Budget Track Options:

- **Budget Track**: $200-400/month = Basic comprehensive preparedness in 18-36 months
- **Standard Track**: $400-800/month = Full comprehensive preparedness in 12-24 months
- **Accelerated Track**: $800-1,500/month = Advanced preparedness in 6-12 months

Total Investment Ranges:

- **Basic Preparedness**: $7,200-14,400 over 18-36 months
- **Comprehensive Preparedness**: $15,000-30,000 over 12-24 months
- **Advanced Preparedness**: $25,000-50,000 over 6-18 months

The Ultimate Goal: Budget-phased implementation makes comprehensive family preparedness accessible to families at all income levels while ensuring every dollar spent provides maximum security value. The systematic approach builds both capability and knowledge over time, creating preparedness that becomes a natural part of family life rather than a financial burden.

Preparedness investment represents the best possible insurance policy—one that provides daily peace of mind while building long-term family security and resilience. The phased approach makes this investment manageable while ensuring comprehensive protection for your family's future.

www.ingramcontent.com/pod-product-compliance
Lightning Source LLC
Chambersburg PA
CBHW050856240426
43673CB00008B/262